For Dan Herr

THE DOROTHY DAY BOOK

EDITED BY
MARGARET QUIGLEY
AND MICHAEL GARVEY

TEMPLEGATE PUBLISHERS

ISBN 0-87243-204-1

Published by
Templegate Publishers
302 East Adams Street
P.O. Box 5152
Springfield, Illinois
62705-5152

INTRODUCTION

In the winter of 1948, while he was visiting New York, Evelyn Waugh wrote to his wife, Laura, about a trip "to the slums to see Dorothy Day, an autocratic saint who wants us all to be poor, and her young men who are poor already & have a paper called *The Catholic Worker* and a soup kitchen." Waugh invited "Mrs. Day" and her young men to have lunch with him at an Italian restaurant on the Lower East Side, noting that "she didn't at all approve of their having cocktails or wine but they had them & we talked till four o'clock."

What a remarkable conversation that must have been.

It is difficult to imagine a pair of world-views more disparate, of personalities more certain to clash, and of intellectual appetites more voracious. Sharing antipasto and Bardolino in that turbulent neighborhood, the lone upholder of western aristocracy (who regarded most Americans as barbarians) and a fierce opponent of the economic system which alone protected his fragile privilege, could not even agree on the menu.

They had two significant things in common, however. The first was their mutual love of literature. (Dorothy Day, in fact, is said to have counted Waugh among her favorite novelists.) The second, and far more important, assured a concord beside which their considerable differences of opinion became trivial, even funny.

That, of course, is the Church, the institution, the family, the tradition, and the Person without which life, for both of them, would simply not have been worth living. Both of them, from entirely dissimilar experiences, had come to the Church after long and costly pilgrimages. Both of them, in entirely dissimilar ways, had embraced the Church passionately. Both of them had submitted to Church authority, never uncritically, but always with a disconcerting humility. That was one other thing they had in common: submission was not a thing which came naturally to either of them.

If Dorothy disapproved the encouragement Waugh gave her co-workers to drink, she would have more vehemently disapproved his description of herself as a saint, even an autocratic one. It was not only that she knew enough about sanctity to dislike its casual attribution, but that she knew enough about her co-religionists to dislike the sentimentality that too often accompanied their praise. She often said that she did not want "to be dismissed so easily."

Her faith gave Dorothy Day humility, and her humility taught her the need for courage. She sought courage in the lives of the saints, and she loved those lives, craving their adventure and light. She loved the Church they comprised, too, "not for itself, because it was so often a scandal to me . . . I loved the Church for Christ made visible."

Dorothy's humility was not saccharine acquiesence but a sort of sanctified "earthiness." It was a force to transform a complicated character without erasing a personality. An observer as perceptive as Waugh might well discern autocracy along with saintliness in "Mrs. Day." If a sophisticated, impatient, impulsive and independent woman hears and heeds the Gospel, the Church must include a sophisticated, impatient, impulsive and independent apostle. What we revere in the life of a saint (and in the life of a Dorothy Day) is not idiosyncrasy, but the Person of Christ, living, working, loving, and revealed in the particulars of that life. He told us that He would remain with us always; the lives of certain people reassure us that His promise is good.

But the particulars remain, fascinating us and telling us much about the sorts of places in which Christ likes to live. From their oddity we can all draw courage, even as Dorothy did, learning that in every personality

— even that weird one of ours — there is a home for God, Who yearns for us like a lover for a lover.

Some of Dorothy Day's particulars: She called for a revolution, a complete reconstruction of society from the ground up. Since Christ was not "visible" in the structures of societal institutions (literally) to hell with them, even if such rejection meant poverty, precarious uncertainty, and long periods in jail. She once referred to the collapse of the Papal States as "an act of divine providence." Although she supported the gravediggers' union in a 1949 strike against the New York Archdiocese (ignoring Cardinal Spellman's denunciation of the strike as "an anti-American, anti-Christian evil, a strike against the Church . . .") she was doctrinally fastidious enough to say that she would "gladly" obey His Eminence if he ordered her to halt publication of her paper and close down her houses of hospitality. "There are many ways," she couldn't help adding, "to handle a Cardinal." The representative of magisterial authority was her spiritual superior; the employer who overworked and underpaid his employees was her foe, churchman or not. She revered priests and despised clericalism. She would enthusiastically break unjust Federal Law (she once told a bewildered IRS auditor, "You figure out how much I owe you and I won't pay it. How's that?"), but she would be horrified to neglect her Easter Duty. An arch-conservative from her mantilla down to her rosary beads, she disliked many of the liturgical changes brought about by the Second Vatican Council. Tom Cornell incurred her wrath for staying too late in the room of his fiancee; Dorothy's attitudes toward the arms race and the sexual revolution were roughly identical.

Once a chain-smoker, she prayed for the desire to quit smoking, received it, and quit. (She was less successful with her caffeine addiction and never travelled anywhere without a jar of instant coffee in her purse.)

3

But the particular which most concerns this book is that she read. Lord, did she read!

Not just the expected bibliography of Christian revolution, either; along with Berdyaev, Pascal, Tolstoy, and Chesterton, she read the Lives of the Saints, literary gossip, Berlitz language courses, Murray Kempton, Dickens, Henry Miller, Dorothy Sayers, D.H. Lawrence, garden columns and, apparently, any travel book she could get her hands on. She read back issues of *The Wall Street Journal* and the *Christian Science Monitor*, gleaned by a roomate from the trashcans of Manhattan. Reading was not only an activity she thoroughly enjoyed (and she was fond of quoting Teresa of Avila: "One must do *some*thing to make life bearable.") but a wellspring of the spiritual life which her vocation both engendered and required:

The books will always be there. If we give up many other distractions, we can turn to them. We can browse among the millions of words written and often just what we find can nourish us, enlighten us, strengthen us — in fact, be our food just as Christ, The Word, is also our food.

The purpose of this book is to provide some examples of those words and, we hope, a taste of that Food. We've undertaken a random and undisciplined reconnaissance of old *Catholic Worker* issues, spoken with many of Dorothy's friends and associates, and culled some excerpts from letters she wrote. This is not, obviously, a thorough anthology, and while every effort has been made to secure permission, we may have failed in a few cases to trace the copyright holder. We apologize for any apparent negligence. Our intention has been to give a sense of the diversity of spiritual and secular reading which nourished both Dorothy Day's spirituality and the Catholic Worker phenomenon.

The principal source of these quotations is the widely known "On Pilgrimage" column, but quotations from elsewhere in Dorothy's paper occasionally appear as well. Readers unfamiliar with the *Catholic Worker* may be surprised by the ease with which a passage from Edmund Wilson shares page space with a passage from Pope Gregory the Great, especially in a periodical which even today fights inflation at a penny a copy. Readers acquainted with the paper and the loose confederation of Catholic Worker houses (roughly fifty at last count) which it concerns should enjoy the recognition of what John Cort noticed when he first encountered the Catholic Worker's matriarch:

"I remember sitting in that dingy hall and saying to myself, 'This woman is getting a lot of fun out of life and I would like to get some of that for myself, so maybe I'd better try the same kind of life.' As much as anything it was a quality of humor and laughter, but with a deeper base than you might expect from a good comedian. It was a humor and laughter that seemed to reach down to the secret, hidden places of the soul, promising ... any minute to explain the mysteries of life and human striving."

Whatever had contributed to this outlook we thought would be worth exploring.

MARGARET QUIGLEY
MICHAEL GARVEY

In the following text the italicized quotations are from Dorothy Day. The woodcuts are by Ade Bethune, a respected and beloved friend of Dorothy Day. Her work has appeared for many years in the Catholic Worker.

He made the earth first and peopled it with dumb creatures, and then He created man to be His overseer on the earth and to hold suzerainty over the earth and the animals on it in His name, not to hold for himself and his descendants inviolable title forever, generation after generation, to the oblongs and squares of the earth, but to hold the earth mutual and intact in the communal anonymity of brotherhood, and all the fee He asked was pity and humility and sufferance and endurance and the sweat of his face for bread. □ WILLIAM FAULKNER

Let me, if I may, be ever welcomed to my room in winter by a glowing hearth, in summer by a vase of flowers; if I may not, let me then think how nice they would be, and bury myself in my work. I do not think that the road to contentment lies in despising what we have not got. Let us acknowledge all good, all delight that the world holds, and be content without it. □ GEORGE MacDONALD

Every moment comes to us pregnant with a command from God, only to pass on and plunge into eternity, there to remain forever what we have made of it. □ ST. FRANCIS DE SALES

It is true that so far as wealth gives time for ideal ends and exercise to ideal energies, wealth is better than poverty and ought to be chosen. But wealth does this in only a portion of the actual cases. Elsewhere the desire to gain wealth and the fear to lose it are our chief breeders of cowardice and propagators of corruption. There are thousands of conjectures in which a wealth-bound man must be a slave, whilst the man for whom poverty has no terrors becomes a freeman. Think of the strength which personal indifference to poverty would give us if we were devoted to unpopular causes. We need no longer hold our tongues or fear to vote the revolutionary or reformatory ticket. Our stocks might fall, our hopes of promotion vanish, our salaries stop, our club doors close in our faces; yet, while we lived, we would imperturbably bear witness to the spirit, and our example would help set free our generation. The cause would need its funds, but we its servants would be potent as we personally were contented with our poverty.

I recommend this matter to your serious pondering, for it is certain that the prevalent fear of poverty among the educated classes is the worst moral disease from which our civilization suffers. ☐ WILLIAM JAMES

The most important acts, both for the one who accomplishes them and for his fellow creatures, are those that have remote consequences. ☐
LEO TOLSTOY

O Lord and Master of my life, take from me the spirit of sloth, faintheartedness, lust of power, and idle talk. But give to Thy servant rather the spirit of chastity, humility, patience, and love. Yea, O Lord and King, grant me to see my own errors and not to judge my brother, for Thou art blessed from all ages to ages. Amen. ☐ EPHRAIM, THE SYRIAN

What more could Christ tell us? In what other way could He more earnestly arouse us to works of mercy or justice, than by telling us that what is given to the needy and the poor is given to Him; and that He is offended when the poor or the needy are denied? So that he who in the Church is not moved by the distress of a brother may be moved by beholding Christ in him, and that he who has no thought for a fellow servant in poverty and need will have a thought for the Lord dwelling in the one whom he turns away.

The means to propitiate God are given us in God's

very words. The divine teachings make clear to us what sinners must do: make satisfaction to God by good works; and that sins are purged away by the rewards of mercy. The Holy Spirit has declared this to us in the psalms: Blessed is he that understands concerning the needy and the poor, for in the day of evil the Lord shall deliver him. ☐ ST. CYPRIAN

I am done with great things and big things, great institutions and big success, and I am for those tiny invisible molecular moral forces that work from individual to individual, creeping through the crannies of the world like so many rootlets, or like the capillary oozing of water, yet which, if you give them time, will rend the hardest monuments of man's pride. ☐ WILLIAM JAMES

Intensified progress seems to be bound up with intensified unfreedom. Throughout the world of industrial civilization the domination of man by man is growing in scope and efficiency. Nor does this trend appear as an incidental, transitory regression on the road to progress. Concentration camps, mass extermination, world wars and atom bombs are no relapse into barbarism, but the unrepressed implementation of the achievements of modern science, technology, and domination. And the most effective subjugation and destruction of man by man takes place at the height of civilization when the material and intellectual attainments of mankind seem to allow the creation of a truly free world. ☐ HERBERT MARCUSE

We live in almost overwhelming danger, at a peak of our apparent control. We react to the danger by attempting to take control, yet we still have to unlearn, as the price of survival, the inherent dominative mode.
□ RAYMOND WILLIAMS

Simone Weil has a message for us here. (I am reading her essays as part of my Lenten reading.) She says that we ". . . must experience every day, both in the spirit and the flesh, the pains and humiliations of poverty . . . and further we must do something which is harder than enduring in poverty, we must renounce all compensations: in our contacts with the people around us we must sincerely practice the humility of a naturalized citizen in the country which has received us."

I keep reminding the young people who come to work with us that they are not naturalized citizens. They cannot get away from their privileged background. They are not really poor. We are always foreigners to the poor. So we have to make up for it by "renouncing all compensations." Simone Weil does not talk of penance, she does not cry out against self-indulgence. She says, "Renounce." In the face of the war in which we are all implicated today, one cannot say less.

This it is whereby the Lord's Passover is duly kept with the unleavened bread of sincerity and truth by the casting away of the old leaven of wickedness and the inebriating and feeding of the new creature with the Lord Himself. For nothing else is brought about by the partaking of the body and blood of Christ than what we pass into that which we then take, and both in spirit and in body carry everywhere Him, in and with Whom we were dead, buried, and rose again. □ ST. LEO THE GREAT

Care enough to be willing to die in order that evil may be overcome. This is the law of the seed, Jesus pointed out, which bears no fruit except it fall into the ground and die. This is the Way of the Cross. □ A. J. MUSTE

How easy it is for me to live with you, O Lord! How easy it is for me to believe in you! When in perplexity, my spirit bares itself or bends. When the most intelligent do not see farther than this evening and do not know what will have to be done tomorrow, you pour into me the serene certitude that you exist and are watching out to see that all the paths of the good not be closed.

On the crest of earthly glory, I consider with astonishment this path through despair. This path from which I myself have been able to send to humanity a reflection of your rays.

All that I shall still have to reflect of them, you will grant me. And what I shall not succeed in reflecting, you have assigned to others. □ ALEXANDER SOLZHENITSYN

Property - the more common it becomes the more holy it becomes. □ ST. GERTRUDE

Piety is allegiance to the will of God. Whether that will is understood or not, it is accepted as good and holy and is obeyed in faith. □ RABBI ABRAHAM HESCHEL

Love without justice is a Christian impossibility, and can only be practiced by those who have divorced religion from life, who dismiss a concern for justice as "politics" and who fear social change much more than they fear God. □ ALAN PATON

Is it wicked to take pleasure in spring and other seasonal changes? To put it more precisely, is it politically reprehensible, while we are all groaning under the shackles of the capitalist system, to point out that life is frequently more worth living because of a blackbird's song, a yellow elm tree in October, or some other natural phenomena which does not cost money and does not have what the editors of the left-wing newspapers call a class angle? □ GEORGE ORWELL

It has become fashionable today to mock or to treat with suspicion, anything which looks like faith in the future. If we are not careful this scepticism will be fatal, for its direct result is to destroy both the love of living and the momentum of mankind. □ TEILHARD DE CHARDIN

Morality is not properly the doctrine of how we may make ourselves happy, but how we may make ourselves worthy of happiness. ☐ IMMANUEL KANT

My Lord God,
I have no idea where I am going.
I do not see the road ahead of me.
I cannot know for certain where it will end.
Nor do I really know myself,
    and the fact that I think that I am following Your will
    does not mean that I am actually doing so.
But I believe that the desire to please You does in fact
    please You.
And I hope that I have that desire in all that I
    am doing.
I hope that I will never do anything apart from that
    desire.
And I know that if I do this,
You will lead me by the right road though I may know
    nothing about it.
Therefore will I trust You always though I may seem to
    be lost and in the shadow of death.
I will not fear, for You are ever with me, and You will
    never leave me to face my perils alone.
☐ THOMAS MERTON

I have observed it in general of those who are fond of scribbling other things, that they are least of all to be depended on for writing letters. God forbid that any of my friends should judge of my regard for them by the punctuality of my correspondence. ☐
EDMUND BURKE

Prayer should be the key of the day and the lock of the night. □ THOMAS FULLER

O Raphael, lead us toward those we are waiting for, those who are waiting for us. Raphael, Angel of Happy Meetings, lead us by the hand toward those we are looking for. May all our movements be guided by your light and transfigured with your Joy. Angel, guide of Tobias, lay the request we now address to you at the feet of Him on whose unveiled Face you are privileged to gaze. Lonely and tired, crushed by the separations and sorrows of life, we feel the need of calling you and of pleading for the protection of your wings, so that we may not be as strangers in the province of joy, all ignorant of the concerns of our country. Remember the weak, you who are strong, you whose home lies beyond the region of thunder, in a land that is always peaceful, always serene and bright with the resplendent glory of God. □ ERNEST HELLO

A single grateful thought towards heaven is the most complete prayer. □ LESSING

He prayeth well who loveth well
Both man and bird and beast
He prayeth best who loveth best
All things both great and small;
For the dear God who loveth us,
He made and loveth all.
□ S. T. COLERIDGE

When the last sea is sailed and the last shallow
    charted.
When the last field is reaped and the last harvest
    stored,
When the last fire is out and the last guest departed.
Grant the last prayer that I shall pray, Be good to me,
    O Lord.
☐ JOHN MASEFIELD

Abide with me from morn till eve,
For without Thee I cannot live;
Abide with me when night is nigh,
For without Thee I dare not die.
☐ JOHN KEBLE

Not what we wish, but what we want,
    Oh! let thy grace supply,
The good unasked, in mercy grant;
    The ill, though ask'd, deny.
☐ JAMES MERRICK, *Hymn*

It is a fact, confirmed and re-confirmed during two or
three thousand years of religious history, that the
ultimate Reality is not clearly and immediately
apprehended, except by those who have made themselves loving, pure in heart and poor in spirit. ☐
ALDOUS HUXLEY in *The Perennial Philosophy*

No man ever prayed heartily without learning something. □ EMERSON

This morning to ward off the noise I have my radio on — Berlioz, Schubert, Chopin, etc. It is not a distraction, it is a pacifier. As St. Teresa of Avila said as she grabbed her castanets and started to dance during the hour of recreation in her unheated convent, "One must do something to make life bearable!"

You are not making a gift of your possessions to the poor person. You are handing over to him what is his. For what has been given in common for the use of all, you have arrogated to yourself. The world is given to all, and not only to the rich. □ ST. AMBROSE

Those who make private property of the gifts of God pretend in vain to be innocent, for in thus retaining the subsistence of the poor, they are the murderers of those who die every day for want of it. □ POPE ST. GREGORY THE GREAT

"Pour forth we beseech Thee, O Lord, Thy grace into our hearts, so that we to whom the Incarnation of Christ, Thy Son, was made known by the message of an Angel, may by His passion and cross be brought to the glory of His resurrection.

"Better be careful when you say that prayer," I told her (Peggy Baird). "God takes us at our word." I was quoting two people actually. John McKeon once said, "Does anyone mean what he is saying?" And Fr. Pacifique Roy said, "God takes us at our word."

Who is the covetous man? One for whom plenty is not enough. Who is the defrauder? One who takes away what belongs to everyone. And are not you covetous, are not you a defrauder, when you keep for private use what you were given for distribution? When someone strips a man of his clothes we call him a thief. And one who might clothe the naked and does not — should not he be given the same name? The bread in your hoard belongs to the hungry; the cloak in your wardrobe belongs to the naked; the shoes you let rot belong to the barefoot; the money in your vaults belongs to the destitute. All you might help and do not — to all these you are doing wrong. □ BASIL THE ELDER

Everything is a grace . . . everything is the direct effect of our Father's love - difficulties, contradictions, humiliations, all the soul's miseries, her burdens, her needs - everything, because through them she learns humility, realizes her weakness. Everything is a grace because everything is God's gift. Whatever be the character of life or its unexpected events — to the heart that loves, all is well. □ ST. THERESE OF LISIEUX

If a thousand men were not to pay their tax bill this year, that would not be a violent and bloody measure as it would be to pay them and enable the State to commit violence and shed innocent blood. □
HENRY DAVID THOREAU

I was delighted to see this rural house of hospitality [which a Fr. McVey had established in a deserted TB hospital in Pulaski, New York] where worker and student, young and old work together to realize St. Catherine's dictum: "All the way to heaven is heaven, because He said, I am the Way."

. . . I have two apologies to make, first for a letter, hastily dictated and not read, which I wrote before in answer to Bob La Sala's letter from International House asking what was to be the topic of my talk at the college. I had dictated something Vinoba Bhava had written, "to teach others, it is good to speak of saints and heroes." In the letter, it had turned into "saints and eros." Puzzled but trustful, the students handed out this title to the press and we had quite a large audience!

Unless I am much mistaken, the Golden Rule is still the same: invest where the profits are highest, quickest and safest. If that means crushing a few, or many, or numerous human beings, it is regrettable, but, the reasoning goes, that is the inevitable price of progress.
□ ARCHBISHOP HELDER CAMARA

Rabbi Leib, son of Sarah, the hidden zaddik who wandered over the earth, following the course of rivers, in order to redeem the souls of the living and the dead, said this: "I did not go to the maggid (teacher) in order to hear Torah from him, but to see how he unlaces his felt shoes and laces them up again." □ MARTIN BUBER in *Tales of the Hasidim*

I am glad that Edmund Wilson brings out the fact that Solzhenitsyn is sincerely religious, and he concedes that it is this man's religious faith that is responsible for his survival. He quotes a few lines of a prayer which has not been published except in a religious paper in France, and which, Wilson says "sounds authentic." This prayer reads as though Solzhenitsyn were writing a letter to the God whom he, by this writing, acknowledges publicly as the object of his faith and hope. It expresses his faith too that God will raise up others, where he has not succeeded, to bring to others the "serene certitude that You exist and that You are watching out to see that all the paths of the good be not closed."

The poor are an easy audience to gull, when you know how to go about it . . . Nothing easier, come to think of it, than to make them feel poverty as a shameful illness, unworthy of a civilized country, that we are going to get rid of the filthy thing in no time. But which one of us would dare to speak thus of the poverty of Jesus Christ? □ GEORGES BERNANOS in *Diary of a Country Priest*

We call ourselves Christian, we citizens of the United States, the majority of us, but no one would ever know us as Christians. Reflect on the life of Jesus who came to call sinners, Who was born in poverty, Who lived as a worker for thirty years. He was an itinerant teacher, walking the roads of Palestine, Who hungered and thirsted and was fatigued to the point of exhaustion, Who was tempted in all things like us, but He did not sin, because He was also God. As the apostles said, we are called to be other-Christs, we are called to put off the old man and put on Christ, we are told to see Christ in our brother. Hard sayings and who can understand it? Only the Spirit can teach us. It is some comfort to remember those further words, when Christ Himself died because His whole way of life was revolutionary — He spoke them from the torture in which He hung, nailed as He was to a cross — "Father, forgive them for they know not what they do." And He also said to the thief dying by His side, "This day thou shalt be with Me in Paradise."

. . . I am afraid of what is before us, because what we sow we will reap. It is an exercise in courage to write these words, to speak in this way when it is revolting to consider how much we profess and how little we perform. God help us. □ EDITORIAL ON THE ATTICA MASSACRE, 1971

We go step by step, I spent four or five years working with these two hands, using a hoe. I worked with the people. We brought pressure, and we kept at it, and now the Mafia no longer controls the water in our area, and the dam is there. It's not that the Mafia is so strong. It's that men are weak as long as they're isolated . . .

There are moments when things go well and one feels encouraged. There are difficult moments and one feels overwhelmed. But it's senseless to speak of optimism or pessimism. The only important thing is to know that if one works well in a potato field, the potatoes will grow. If one works well among men, they will grow. That's reality. The rest is smoke. It's important to know that words don't move mountains. Work, exacting work, moves mountains." □ DANILO DOLCI

St. Augustine (to whom Paul Goodman was rather startlingly compared, it seemed to me, because of his public confession) wrote in The City of God, "All men are members or potential members of the Body of Christ." So we should look upon them as such. If in some ways they are opponents, or at least inimical on some issues (like sex) — well, Jesus told us to love our enemies, many of whom are not of our own dear household. He also told us not to judge. Hard sayings.

Fr. Zachary, God rest his soul, a priest at the Church of Our Lady of Guadalupe on 14th Street, said to me years ago, "There is no time with God." And he told me to pray "in the future" for an 18-year old friend who had committed suicide. "Since there is no time with God, your prayers now will have called down the grace of a happy death. At the moment of death that boy will have been given the choice of light or darkness, beauty or ugliness, peace or endless horror."

There is a terrible saying a priest once quoted to us, "He who says he has done enough has already perished." If we went daily to our local church, and there, in the presence of Christ, brought our problems, our pain, our suffering at our failures, and our mistakes which contribute so much to the sufferings of others, then I think we would more nearly be doing "enough." The growth of prayer groups all over the country does not mean a slackening of the struggle for peace and justice, but a strengthening of it.

During the darkest periods of history, quite often a small number of men and women, scattered throughout the world, have been able to reverse the course of historical evolutions. This was only possible because they hoped beyond all hope. What had been bound for disintegration then entered into the current of a new dynamism. □ ROGER SCHUTZ, ABBOT OF TAIZE

Rabbi Mendel said: "I don't know wherein I could be better than the worm. For see: he does the will of his Maker and destroys nothing." □ MARTIN BUBER in *Tales of the Hasidim*

The books will always be there. If we give up many other distractions, we can turn to them. We can browse among the millions of words written and often just what we find can nourish us, enlighten us, strengthen us — in fact, be our food just as Christ, the Word, is also our food.

Modern investigators of miraculous history have solemnly admitted that a characteristic of the great saints is their power of "levitation." They might go further; a characteristic of the great saints is their power of levity. Angels can fly because they can take themselves lightly. □ G.K. CHESTERTON

At the bottom of the heart of every human being, from earliest infancy until the tomb, there is something that goes on indomitably expecting, in the teeth of all experience of crimes committed, suffered, and witnessed, that good and not evil will be done to him. It is this above all that is sacred in every human being. □ SIMONE WEIL

To be a witness does not consist in engaging in propaganda, nor even in stirring people up, but in being a living mystery. It means to live in such a way that one's life would not make sense if God did not exist. □ CARDINAL SUHARD

When we are able to bear some small share of the sufferings of the world, whether in pain of mind, body or soul, let us thank God for that too. Maybe we are helping some prisoner, some black or Puerto Rican youth in the Tombs, some soldier in Vietnam. The old I.W.W. slogan, "An injury to one is an injury to all," is another way of saying what St. Paul said almost two thousand years ago. "We are all members of one another, and when the health of one member suffers, the health of the whole body is lowered." And the converse is true. We can indeed hold each other up in prayer. Excuse this preaching. I am preaching to myself too.

Recall the face of the poorest and the most helpless man whom you may have seen and ask yourself if the step you contemplate is going to be of any use to him. Will he be able to gain anything by it? Will it restore him to a control over his own life and destiny? In other words, will it lead to the swaraj or self rule for the hungry and the spiritually starved millions of our fellow men. If so then you will find your doubts and yourself melting away. □ THE GANDHI TALISMAN

As for me, I have been going to bed at dark. If I put the reading lamp on, the little porch where I sleep swarms with all kinds of insects that fly in your eyes, your hair, your nose, your ears, and then in your mouth if you leave it open. I have been pestered with all kinds of insects, remembering St. Benedict Joseph Labre, the derelict saint of Rome, who slept in doorways and disregarded his vermin . . . there is also St. Francis Xavier. When he was in the Indies, St. Ignatius wrote, begging news of how it was going with his lonely apostle at the other end of the world. "I am interested to hear even of the fleas that bite you," he wrote. And, of course, speaking of fleas, there was St. Teresa of Avila whose convent was plagued once with some kind of insect and she wrote a song which her nuns sang in procession, a song of petition, and was never afflicted again.

I don't remember the time when I was not writing a book.

Only he who learns to love men one by one reaches, in his relation to heaven, God as the God of all the world . . . For he learns to love the God of the universe, the God who loves His work, only in the measure in which he himself learns to love the world. □ MARTIN BUBER

The real sin of idolatry is always committed on behalf of something similar to the State. It was this sin that the devil wanted Christ to commit when he offered Him the kingdoms of this world. Christ refused. Richelieu accepted . . . The Romans really were an atheistic and idolatrous people, not idolatrous with regard to images made of stone or bronze, but idolatrous with regard to themselves. It is this idolatry that they have bequeathed to us in the form of patriotism. □ SIMONE WEIL

Christianity should be the alternative to Caesar, and so intent in its virtue that Caesar will not be able to stand in the strength of its light. □ JULIUS LESTER

ST·ELISABETH

TAKES·CARE
OF·THE·SICK

If the Gospel appeals to you, it is easy to come out against general social injustice, against the exploitation of the poor, in favor of pacifism, ethical vegetarianism or other isms. But it is a thousand times harder to tackle problems of hostility, coldness, or injustice in the relationships with those with whom you are in contact everyday. It is also much less spectacular. ☐ KARL STERN

Buddhists teach that a man's life is divided into three parts: the first part for education and growing up; the second for continued learning, of course, through marriage and raising a family, involvement with the life of the senses, the mind and the spirit; and the third period, the time of withdrawal from responsibility, letting go of the things of this life, letting God take over. This is a fragmentary view of the profound teaching of the East. The old saying that man works from sun to sun, but woman's work is never done is a very true one. St. Teresa wrote of the three interior senses, the memory, the understanding and the will, so even if one withdraws, as I am trying to do, from active work, these senses remain active.

If you do away with the yoke, the clenched fist, the wicked word, if you give your bread to the hungry, and relief to the oppressed, your light will rise in darkness and your shadows become like noon. Yahweh will give strength to your bones, and you shall be like a watered garden, like a spring of water which never runs dry. ☐ ISAIAH 58

The disease was this — that Christians who would be horrified to have their devotion to Jesus questioned did not in fact find him very interesting. □ FRANK SHEED

I *shall start it [her "On Pilgrimage" column] again with two quotations which somehow clarified the situation, our life and our work for me. The first is from Jan Adam's last article in the CW, "Farm Workers in Perspective." She writes, "There does not seem to be any dynamism inherent in the mere existence of a meaningful social alternative that enables all people to make it more than an insulated haven." The other quote is from "Signs in the Wind," in New Blackfriars, by Rosemary Haughton. "It is this earthy spirituality that Christians need to recover if the Church is to be prophetic, wild and holy, and not merely socially enlightened . . . it is time to take the lid once more off the well of truth from which the mystics and saints drew."*

It is important to preserve the mind's chastity . . . Think of admitting the details of a single case of the criminal court into our thoughts, to stalk profanely through their very sanctum sanctorum for an hour, ay for many hours! to make a very barroom of the mind's inmost apartment, as if for so long the very dust of the street had occupied us — the very street itself, with all its travel, its bustle, and filth, had passed through our heart's shrine. Would it not be an intellectual and moral suicide? □ HENRY DAVID THOREAU

Perhaps peace is not, after all, something you work for, or fight for . . . Peace is something you have or do not have. If you are yourself at peace, then there is at least some peace in the world . . . I am not speaking of quietism, because quietism is not peace, nor is it the way to peace. □ THOMAS MERTON

All voting is a sort of gaming, like checkers, or backgammon, a playing with right and wrong; its obligation never exceeds that of expediency. Even voting for the right thing is doing nothing for it. A wise man will not leave the right to the mercy of chance, nor wish it to prevail through the power of the majority. □ HENRY DAVID THOREAU

Pluck up thy courage, faint heart; what though thou be fearful, sorry and weary, and standest in great dread of most painful torments, be of good comfort; for I Myself have vanquished the whole world, and yet I have felt far more fear, sorrow, weariness, and much more inward anguish, too, when I considered My most bitter, painful Passion to press so fast upon Me. He that is stronghearted may find a thousand glorious, valiant martyrs whose example he might right joyously follow. But thou, now, O timorous and weak, silly sheep, think it sufficient for thee only to walk after Me, Which am thy Shepherd and Governor, and so mistrust thyself and put thy trust in Me. Take hold on the hem of My garment, therefore; from thence shalt thou perceive such strength and relief to proceed. □ THOMAS MORE

Today is the feast of St. Nicholas of Tolentine, who preached sermons on the street corner, my missal says. I still use a missal because I want to hold fast to those prayers in the canon of the Mass, and because I want to know the feasts, the saints, and heroes we celebrate; also sometimes the priest is not a clear speaker. Yesterday was the feast of St. Peter Claver who is the patron of all the priests who work with the Negro and who struggle for civil rights, who hunger and thirst after justice, and the epistle and the Gospel are inspiring. The Maryknoll missal has all the psalms and there is a prayer for every occasion, the prayer of the Israelite, the prayer of the Christian.

Far from demanding that the lunatic race for destruction be stepped up, it seems to me that Christian morality imposes on every single one of us the obligation to protest against it and to work for the creation of an international authority with power and sanctions that will be able to control technology, and divert our amazing virtuosity into the service of man instead of against him.

It is not enough to say that we ought to try to work for a negotiated disarmament, or that one power block or the other ought to take the lead and disarm unilaterally. Methods and policies can and should be fairly considered. But what matters most is the obligation to travel in every feasible way in the direction of peace, using all the traditional and legitimate methods, while at the same time seeking to improvise new and original measures to achieve our end. □ THOMAS MERTON

Force in the hands of another exercises over the soul the same tyranny that extreme hunger does; for it possesses, and in perpetuo, the power of life and death. Its rule, moreover, is as cold and hard as the rule of inert matter. The man who knows himself weaker than another is more alone in the heart of the city than a man lost in the desert. ☐ SIMONE WEIL

You do not enter into paradise tomorrow or the day after or in ten years; you enter it today when you are poor and crucified. ☐ LEON BLOY

St. Thomas said once that he learned more by prayer than he did by study, and it is only prayer that will give us a full life of joy, a word which Bernanos and C.S. Lewis alike took as meaning more than "happiness."

A deep abiding joy can only be ours if we emphasize the "primacy of the spiritual," a phrase which Peter Maurin loved. We must grow in faith, in our spiritual capacity to "do all things in Him Who strengthens us," even change the social order so that wars will cease and it will be easier to be good, to keep our sanity, be whole men, holy men, and truly love one another. If men can walk on the moon, why not?

If we were followers of Jesus, we too could multiply loaves and fishes and save the world. "It all goes together," Eric Gill wrote years ago.

It helped me greatly to read once in one of Saroyan's stories of an Armenian household and a family squabble where the father and two sons began knocking each other around and the mother of the house calmly going on serving the dessert. "Food hath charms to soothe the savage breast." I am misquoting of course, and exaggerating, speaking in hyperbole, but the foundation of hospitality is — "They knew Him in the breaking of the bread." The very word "companion" means one you break bread with.

Personally I do not favor violence, because of my religious convictions. Christ taught peace. I believe in the force of liberating moral pressure. But many young people are disillusioned with the possibilities of nonviolence. They tell me that all we have done is wasted, and that the Church still only speaks in platitudes. They say the only remaining way is the violent way. I reply to them that a future of ten or fifteen years of violence is in itself a waste, even by their own criteria. □ ARCHBISHOP HELDER CAMARA

Back of every creation, supporting it like an arch, is faith. Enthusiasm is nothing: it comes and goes. But if one believes, then miracles occur. Faith has nothing to do with profits: if anything, it has to do with prophets. Men who know and believe can foresee the future. They don't want to put something over — they want to put something under us. They want to give solid support to our dreams. The world isn't kept running because it's a paying proposition. (God doesn't make a cent on the deal.) The world goes on because a few men in every generation believe in it utterly, accept it unquestioningly; they underwrite it with their lives. In the struggle which they have to make themselves understood they create music; taking the discordant elements of life, they weave a pattern of harmony and significance. If it weren't for this constant struggle on the part of a few creative types to expand the sense of reality in man the world would literally die out. We are not kept alive by legislators and militarists; that's fairly obvious. We are kept alive by men of faith, men of vision. They are like vital germs in the endless process of becoming. Make room, then, for the life-giving ones! □ HENRY MILLER

The artist, the man who makes, is less important to mankind, for good and evil, than the apostle, the man with a message. Without religion, a philosophy, a code of behaviour, call it what you will, men cannot live at all: what they believe may be absurd or revolting, but they have to believe something. On the other hand, however much the arts may mean to us, it is possible to imagine our lives without them. □ W.H. AUDEN

Loving begins loving; then, love will start. Self dies, then rises in another heart. □ JOHN FANDEL

Sometimes our hearts are heavy with the tragedy of the world, the horrible news from Vietnam, Brazil, Biafra, the Israeli-Arab war. And here it is Advent and Christmas time again, and with it the juxtaposition of joy and sorrow, the blackness of night, brightness of dawn. What saves us from despair is a phrase we read in The Life of Jesus by Daniel-Rops, "getting on with the business of living." What did the women do after the crucifixion? The men were in the upper room mourning and praying and the women, by their very nature, "had to go on with the business of living." They prepared the spices, purchased the linen cloths for the burial, kept the Sabbath, and hastened to the tomb on Sunday morning. Their very work gave them insights as to time, and doubtless there was a hint of the peace and joy of resurrection to temper their grief.

"Deal your bread to the hungry and take those without shelter into your house," we are told at the beginning of Lent. That has meant that we have grown into a community of sorts, and somehow or other the Lord has blessed us and sent us what we needed over the years. But He told us to ask. "Ask and you shall receive, seek and you shall find, knock and it shall be opened to you." I love those words and recommend them to all. Pascal even elaborated on the second part and put the words into the mouth of Our Lord, "You would not seek Me if you had not already found Me," thinking, I suppose, that there is no time with God . . . but again, I repeat, it is not a destitution, but a sharing which the Lord Jesus enables us to do . . . What need of foundation funds or government funds, to do what work we do? St. Hilary commented once, "The less we have of Caesar's, the less we will have to render to Caesar."

Thank God we have some heroes today in the social field whose vision illuminates the hard work they propose. Most of our aims are too small. I often think of St. Teresa of Avila, who said that we compliment God by asking great things of Him, and I do ask Him to make this vision of Saul Alinsky grow in the minds of the men who hear Him . . .

. . . the book I remember of his is Reveille for Radicals, published twenty or more years ago and which tells most vividly of the Back of the Yards movement in Chicago . . . since my own radical interests were sparked by Upton Sinclair's book, The Jungle, Alinsky's book interested me, and because he thought in terms of building from the ground up, rather than from the top down, on the principle of subsidiarity.

Anyway, give me the simple old-fangled bohemian in his garret. Nine times out of ten, he was incompetent in the business of life; but this very poverty prevented him from sinking into real decadence — which is the loss of an object in life. ☐ RUSSELL KIRK

My roommate Marie . . . used to gather newspapers from the trash receptacles all over the city every afternoon and come back in the evening to give us our choice. We didn't have much choice last month. I ask her for The Wall Street Journal, but she doesn't often get that. The few copies I saw in this time of dearth fascinate me. One issue told all about how complicated is the life of Roy Cohn, who prosecuted Alger Hiss and who is, or rather was, our staunch defender against communism . . . Silence would be the only weapon against such an opponent as Cohn. Anyway, his affairs seem to be very complicated now and he is mixed up in all kinds of ownership of businesses, all of which was set forth by the Wall Street Journal in a front page right hand column and perhaps a Balzac could understand it but I could not . . . I ask Marie for the Christian Science Monitor too, as there are nature notes and feature articles about Maine and New England and rural life which make very pleasant reading in the New York slums . . . She has the Post now. Murray Kempton doesn't work there anymore, but there are some interesting stories about a woman with eighteen cats and how she was sent away to a mental hospital, and about a vagrant who was picked up with $50,000 on him. There is so much happening . . .

What cheers me in my study [of Spanish] is remembering what Raissa Maritain wrote about how she sat as a little girl, miserable in her French classrooms when her family first came from Russia to France and how suddenly she began to understand.

The next day was the feast of the Assumption, which always reminds me of that saying of St. Augustine's - "The flesh of Jesus is the flesh of Mary," and emphasizes to me the dignity of her humanity, just as the feast of the Sacred Heart emphasizes the love of God for man. The feast of the Assumption together with the doctrine of the resurrection of *the body makes heaven real, and goodness knows we need to grow in faith and in hope of heaven in this perilous life which we nevertheless so treasure and cling to.*

The stalemate must be broken, but it will never be broken by rational argument. There are too many right reasons for wrong actions on both sides. It can only be broken by instinctive action. An act of disobedience is or should be collectively instinctive — a revolt of the instincts of man against the threat of mass destruction. Instincts are dangerous things to play with, but that is why, in the present desperate situation, we must play with instincts. The apathetic indifference of the majority of people to the very real threat of universal destruction is partly due to a lack of imagination, but the imagination does not function in the present situation because it is paralyzed by fear in its subconscious sources. We must release the imagination of the people so that they become fully conscious of the fate that is threatening them, and we can best reach their imagination by our actions, our fearlessness, by our willingness to sacrifice our comfort, our liberty, and even our lives to the end that mankind shall be delivered from pain and suffering and universal death. □ SIR HERBERT READ

It is almost fifty years of struggle, since at 14 I began to read the class-conscious fiction of Upton Sinclair, who is called the Dickens of America, and Jack London, who is a best seller in Russia, not to speak of the Day Book in Chicago which was a socialist, ad-less newspaper on which Carl Sandburg worked, and one of my brothers also.

If you want an order which is alive and not a dead standardization, you must start from the small unit and go by gradual stages to the large: the individual man and woman finding their life in the home; the home helping to make the life of the village or town; this in its turn helping to form the life of the larger community of district or county or province; and only then coming, through the various contributions of these parts of the nation, to the life of the nation itself, which in its turn has its part to play, its particular gift to bring to the life of the world. □ GERALD VANN, O.P.

St. Catherine of Siena preached a Crusade, saying that it was better to go fight the heathen and regain the Holy Land, than for the Italian cities to be fighting among themselves. And on the other hand our Lord said through her, "I have left Myself in the midst of you, that what you do for these, I will count as done for Myself." And in this she was thinking of the poor.

And St. Teresa of Avila prayed that before her nuns became rich and lived in fine buildings, the walls would fall upon them and crush them. Yet she accepted money from her brothers who went to the New World to make their fortunes. Those fortunes were made by robbing the native populations, enslaving them, even wiping them out completely (after baptizing them and anointing them first, perhaps.) Hard not to be cynical, hard not to judge. Fr. Hugo said that one could go to hell imitating the imperfections of the saints. He also said that we loved God as much as the one we loved the least. What a hard and painful thing it is to love the exploiter. When I was interviewed by Mike Wallace on television, and he asked me, "Do you think God loves a Hitler and a Stalin?" I could only quote, "God loves all men. God wills that all men be saved."

We cannot accept that the murderous course of history is irremediable and that the human spirit that believes in itself cannot influence the most powerful force in the world. The experience of recent generations convinces me that only the unbending human spirit taking its stand on the front line against the violence that threatens it, ready to sacrifice itself and to die proclaiming: not one step further - only this inflexibility of the spirit can be the real defender of personal peace, universal peace, and all humanity. □
ALEXANDER SOLZHENITSYN

In America people frequently say that unilateralism and Christian non-violence will not work against an enemy who is not Christian . . . But in the case of Christians is this not a double standard? Did not the glory of the early Christians shine forth in their adherence to a law of charity utterly at odds with the standards of Roman society? The distinguished Catholic psychiatrist Karl Stern put it in a striking way recently when he suggested that if "there had existed during the time of Christ a powerful aggressor such as the Roman imperial army, equipped with gadgets to get at wombs, at fetuses and even at unborn generations," Christ would not have advocated such instruments by his own people even as a deterrent, but in fact would have demanded "*the acceptance of torture, mutilation, and death rather than even prepare such instruments."*

The real objection of the early Christians to military service is found in the phrase "Ecclesia abhorret a sanguine" — the Church shrinks from bloodshed.

. . . The testimony of the great Christian scholar Origen in the 3rd century is pertinent. Celsus, a cultivated pagan concerned about the crumbling of Rome, criticized the Christians particularly for their refusal to fight in the army. Origen, replying in his famous Contra Celsum, said: "Christians have been taught not to defend themselves against their enemies; and because they have kept the laws which command gentleness and love to man, on this account they have received from God that which they would not have succeeded in doing if they had been given the right to make war, even if they may have been quite able to do so." He always fought for them, and from time to time stopped the opponents of the Christians, and the people who wanted to kill them.

. . . Christian pacifism can find no better definition than in the Contra Celsum: "No longer do we take the sword against other nations, nor do we learn war any more since we have become the sons of peace through Jesus, Who is our author, instead of following the traditional customs by which we were strangers to the covenant."

To be old is a glorious thing when one has not unlearned what it means "to begin." ☐ MARTIN BUBER

. . . How outrageously the principle of noncombatant immunity, which forbids the killing of those not directly engaged in war, has been flouted in modern wars when only so-called conventional weapons have been used may be judged by perusing such a book as Martin Caidin's "The Night Hamburg Died," the horrible story of the "Gomorrah" raid by the RAF in July 1943 on the great German city. An estimated 70,000 people were cooked or asphyxiated in the terrible firestorm that enveloped the doomed metropolis . . . The suffering of the children is described by Caidin in unforgettable words: "Their best, the very substance of their heart and their soul — it is all too little. For they must keep raising and lowering the children, plunging them into the canal water so that the heat radiation will not flay their skins. The children suffer terribly, unable to cry out, gasping for breath . . . sucking in the terrible heated air when they are thrust upward. Their hair steams. Their tongues are swollen and they cannot cry . . ." WWII demonstrates how inevitably military expediency pushes aside moral restraints.

T hat work applies to the spirit and the spirit to work can be seen in two of the classic religious rules which influenced Peter Maurin's thinking — those of St. Benedict and St. Francis. Both speak of the right relationships of prayer to work. St. Benedict's "Ora et Labora" speaks of the necessity of daily labor. And Francis dedicates the fifth chapter of his Rule to work, and, we are told, dismissed one of the lazy friars as "Brother Fly." ☐ MICHAEL DE GREGORY

God wills that all men be saved. A hard saying for us to take and believe and hold to our heart to ease its bitterness. St. John of the Cross wrote, "Where there is no love, put love, and you will find love." He was in jail too, put there by his own brethren.

Someday, after mastering the winds, the waves, the tides and gravity, we shall harness for God the energies of love, and then, for the second time in the history of the world, man will discover fire. □ TEILHARD DE CHARDIN

No matter how marvellous our inventions, how productive our industries, how exquisitely automatic our machines, the whole process may be brought to a standstill by its failure fully to engage the human personality or to serve its needs . . . In short: we must do justice to the whole nature of man before we can make the most of our mechanical improvements. □ LEWIS MUMFORD

We say that normally . . . a man finds his greatest interest and pleasure and enthusiasm in his work; that that work to bear him the fruit of interest and pleasure must be work by which he earns his living and not merely work done in his spare time . . .; that such work to bear fruit, must be such as the worker is responsible for, not merely for its lack of faults but for its merits. □ ERIC GILL

When through one man a little more love and goodness, a little more light and truth come into the world, then that man's life has had meaning. □ ALFRED DELP

Into this world, this demented inn, in which there is absolutely no room for Him at all, Christ has come un-invited. But because He cannot be at home in it, be-cause He is out of place in it, His place is with those others for whom there is no room. His place is with those who do not belong, who are rejected by power because they are regarded as weak, those who are discredited, who are denied the status of persons, who are tortured, bombed, and exterminated. With those for whom there is no room, Christ is present in the world. He is mysteriously present in those for whom there seems to be nothing but the world at its worst . . . It is in these that He hides Himself, for whom there is no room. □ THOMAS MERTON

When are laws, customs, institutions right? Only when they tally with the natural and revealed law that God has given us. Our laws are human decrees for ap-plying God's law to our social life, just as the clock is the human device for making the sun's course known and accessible at night and in a cloudy world. If a clock goes fast or slow, its error will accumulate until it will tell us that it is bedtime at dawn. We need to set our clocks by the sun; that is what Greenwich is for. So with our laws and customs. They need to be tested and set again by the sun of justice. As Carlyle said, "If you will have your laws obeyed without mutiny, see well that they be pieces of God Almighty's law." To say that we must fall in with a state of things that is manifestly at variance with God's law is to say that we must rule our lives by the clock, even when it tells us that night is day. □ From GOOD WORK (*Formerly the Catholic Art Quarterly*)

Today, May second, Caryl Chessman was gassed to death at San Quentin, California, after a twelve-year fight to save his life. Eight times he was brought to the death cell and eight times he was given a last minute reprieve. To have some idea of the torture this man went through, one should read The Idiot, by Dostoievsky, in which the author tells the story of how he himself was brought to the verge of death and at the last moment his sentence was commuted. Personally, we believe in the innocence of Chessman. But be he innocent or guilty, we are opposed to capital punishment. One hundred students walked from the university at Berkeley and from San Francisco and kept vigil all last night. What with the prayers we have said and the fasting Bob Steed (an Associate Editor of the Catholic Worker) did for the last forty-six days we have no doubt that at the end Chessman turned to Light rather than darkness. May God grant his tormented soul rest and a place of pardon.

The system of private property is no more absolutely immutable than any other human institution and history shows it. □ POPE PIUS XI

Since her institution the Catholic Church has never ceased at every point of the globe and every instant of her duration to have difficulties with every form of society and of the state, even of those which seemed to borrow from her their constituent principles.

No government will find Christians in revolt, but what is worse, it will find them profoundly indifferent. It feels a dull irritation on hearing there is in a Christian soul something that does not belong to it, something which is not for it, and fundamentally escapes it.

It feels that it is seen through, and that to the very depths of its provisory essence, it is not taken seriously. It feels that it is no longer truly sovereign but a kind of steward or procurator, an overseer of material interests whose services are accepted with a resignation which it is not always difficult to mistake for scorn.
□ PAUL CLAUDEL

The meeting [in Seattle, Wash.] was held on a houseboat named Bilgewater . . . Several proclaimed themselves atheists before the meeting started and the host who was barefooted and bearded was a teacher of mathematics. The meeting was good and the questions intelligent, but one young man who had had a lot of wine kept the meeting to a dialogue which must have been a bore to the rest. When I left he started reading aloud a psychotic poem from Howl, a beatnik magazine . . .

That state is a state of Slavery in which a man does what he likes to do in his spare time and in his working time that which is required of him. □ ERIC GILL

I've been reading a very stimulating book recently, God the Unknown by Fr. Victor White; he says that while you are lifted to great heights of awe and worship contemplating God the Unknown, all that He is not, you are suddenly overwhelmed with thankfulness that He is Love; that, "invisible in His own nature, He becomes visible in ours; incomprehensible, He chose to be comprehended; existing before time began, He begins to exist in time," that, in very truth, Jesus is the "image of God" and He speaks to us.

You say that the war does not prevent personal life from going on, that the individual can still love and be complete. It isn't true. The one quality of love is that it universalizes the individual. If I love, then I am extended over all people, but particularly over my own nation. It is an extending in concentric waves over all people. This is the process of love. And if I love, I, the individual, then necessarily the love extends from me to my nearest neighbor, and outwards, till it loses itself in vast distance. This is love, there is no love but this. So that if I love, the love must beat upon my neighbors, till they too live in the spirit of love, and so on, further and further. And how can this be, in war, when the spirit is against love? □ D. H. LAWRENCE

If science produces no better fruits than tyranny, murder, rapine, and the destitution of national morality, I would rather wish our country to be ignorant, honest, and estimable as our neighboring savages are. □ THOMAS JEFFERSON

Jesus has bought back the world by His suffering and what counts in this world is still suffering. If you suffer you are the best part of society. Above the prisons there are only the convents. Here one suffers; there one prays. It's not true that you may be ostracized by society. You, with your suffering, are at its very core and if you pray you will be at the top. I am your mayor and I like you more than the other citizens of Florence. ☐ GIORGIO LA PIRA [talking to prisoners]

Those conferences [at a Marist retreat which Dorothy and a number of her co-workers took part in] were very stimulating, and I thought of C.S. Lewis's statement that unless the egg develops, unless it hatches and grows wings and flies, it becomes a rotten egg. A homely and startling thought.

I thought, too, of those sad lines of Francis Thompson. "Life is a coquetry of death / which wearies me / too sure of the amour. A tiring room where I / death's divers garments try / till fit some fashion sit. / It seemeth me too much / I do rehearse for such / A mean and single scene." I quote from memory, and am not even sure of my divisions of the lines.

I GIVE THANKS FOR:
Morning, stars I see
In country dark, the sea,
Sun, wind, sky,
Shapes of the moon, high
High hawks, earth,

Seeds, seasons of birth,
Death, breath, mist,
Rocks, brooks which twist,
Meadows, rivers, rain,
Moss, vines, grain,
The divine providence
In sanctities of sense,
And every similar thing
Not in this reckoning,
Sorrow and delight,
Sleep, waking, night.
□ JOHN FANDEL

I bought a copy of Bohemia [while travelling in Cuba, in 1962] a monthly, which is only twenty cents. I opened it to the picture of George Bernard Shaw with the inscription underneath (in Spanish, of course): The United States is the only nation in history which has passed from feudalism to decadence without any intermediate steps.

The task facing us will not be done if our philosophers and theologians continue to live among, work with and speak to people and problems long since dead and buried . . . Here is an age crying for the light and guidance of Christian wisdom. What must future judges think of us if we live in the most exciting age of science ever known to mankind and philosophize mainly about Aristotle's physics? We live today in the threatening shadow of cosmic thermonuclear destruction and often theologize about the morality of war as though the spear had not been superseded by the I.C.B.M. □ THEODORE M. HESBURGH

Lord, help us to be Christ-bearers

*Last week we were reading Helen Waddell's translation of
The Desert Fathers and she writes, "their every action
showed a standard of values which turned the world upside
down. It was their humility, their gentleness, their heart-
breaking courtesy that was the seal of their sanctity."*

*God sees the truth but waits. He waits on us to open our
eyes and ears to justice and charity. Let us be part of His
justice, "whose property it is always to have mercy and to
spare."*

The Cross awaits not only the individual man but
also society as a whole, a State or a civilization . . . In
its application to social life the Cross does not imply an
acceptance of social conditions, but rather an acceptance of the idea of inevitable catastrophe, revolution,
and radical social changes. It is a profound error to regard the Cross in a conservative light. □ NICHOLAS
BERDYAEV

*In his talk to young seminarians Abbe Pierre [of the
Emmaus Community in Paris] begs these future priests to
be haunted by the sufferings of the world. The poor man
needs not a program, not a plan, just food and a home.
But the politician finds it impossible to imagine the
condition of the homeless. In a world where babies die of
cold quite legally — but are kept alive illegally if you have
not the necessary building permits — the Prophet must*

return, standing in poverty near God and proclaiming God's judgement on human indifference.

To convert the poor you must be like them; to convert the rich you must be unlike them.

A break has been created in the Christian conscience between the order of charity, in which everyone strives to attain God, and the political order, which has its own laws — the first of which is based on a refusal to believe that the word of God carries binding moral obligations . . . We were reading the Beatitudes devoutly while blood flowed in Madagascar and Indochina.

Quite unwittingly, we have all remained attentive to another sermon. "Blessed are the strong! Blessed are the hard of heart! Blessed are those who scoff at justice and deliver the innocent to the torturer; who order their police to fire on the poor. For theirs is the kingdom of earth."

Well, no . . . Political wisdom is not separated from that wisdom which was taught from the Mount. When the meek were promised that they would possess the earth and those who thirst after justice that they will have their fill, this promise was also addressed to the nations of the world. ☐ FRANCOIS MAURIAC

Our wishes and desires — to pass an exam, to marry the person we love, to sell our house at a good price — are involuntary and, therefore, not in themselves prayers. They only become prayers when addressed to a God whom we believe to know better than ourselves whether we should be granted or denied what we ask. A petition does not become a prayer unless it ends with the words, spoken or unspoken, "nevertheless not as I will but as Thou wilt." □ W.H. AUDEN

However indisposed to do so at present, we may be compelled, sooner or later, to recognize that true loyalty to genuine religious authority is not synonymous with a passive obedience that entails submission to all authority of whatever kind. What we must be on our guard against is an attitude of unthinking conservatism . . . that seems to have led only too many Christians, and clerics in particular, to look on every successful dictator as sent by Providence. □ FR. LOUIS BOUYER

In the conflict between the dead and living capital, it is the role of the Church to protect the poor, the workers, who have accumulated the riches common to humanity. □ CARDINAL MANNING

Christ may have meant: If you love mankind absolutely you will as a result not care for any possessions whatever, and this seems a very likely proposition. But it is one thing to believe that a proposition is probably true; it is another thing to see it as a fact. If you loved mankind as Christ loved them, you would see His conclusion is a fact. It would be obvious. You would sell your goods and they would be no loss to you. These truths, while literal to Christ, and to any mind that has Christ's love for mankind, become parables to lesser natures. There are in every generation people who, beginning innocently, with no predetermined intention of becoming saints, find themselves drawn into the vortex by their interest in helping mankind, and by the understanding that comes from actually doing it. The abandonment of their old mode of life is like dust in the balance. It is done gradually, incidentally, imperceptibly. Thus the whole question of the abandonment of luxury is no question at all, but a mere incident to another question, namely, the degree to which we abandon ourselves to the remorseless logic of our love for others. ☐ JOHN JAY CHAPMAN

"Let us be kind and orderly," one of the Negro leaders [of the fledgling southern civil rights movement] said, according to the radio one morning, and those words were infinitely touching . . . "Be kind," Ruysbroeck wrote, "be kind, be kind and you will soon be saints." Kindness is the outward expression of love in the heart, and is anything but a mild virtue. In these cases it is heroic. "A kind person is one who acknowledges his kinship with other men and acts upon it, confesses that he owes to them as of one blood with himself the debt of love," wrote Richard Trench.

Love is the responsibility of an I for a you. In this lies the likeness of all who love . . . from the blessedly protected man, whose life is rounded in that of a loved being, to him who is all his life nailed to the cross of the world, and who ventures to bring himself to the dreadful point, to love all men. ☐ MARTIN BUBER

I now believe that my welfare, and that of other people, is only possible when each one labors not for himself, but for others, and not only ceases to withhold his work from others, but gives it to anyone who needs it. □ LEO TOLSTOY

Pacifism is a positive faith; it is the faith of those who believe that men are made for peace and that peace is not only natural to men but is that state of affairs in which alone men can fulfill themselves or (what is only another way of saying the same thing) properly serve their fellow men and love and praise God. □ ERIC GILL

It is a high crime indeed to withdraw allegiance from God in order to please men; an act of consummate wickedness to break the laws of Jesus Christ in order to yield obedience to earthly rulers. □ POPE LEO XIII

The State can kill by kindness. It will kill by kindness if you allow it to turn society into a kindergarten. If you allow it to become something outside society, something to which you are passive . . . if you allow it to do for you things which it is part of your human life of making to do for yourself, then you lose your heritage, even though you lose it so gradually that you fail to notice your loss. The first stage is to sink into selfishness and forget the ideal of a common work . . . The second stage follows inevitably: you treat it as a matter of course that the State should take over from you the work not only of building society, but even of the making of our own life. You will be killed not by State tyranny, but by social service. □ GERALD VANN, O.P.

Non-violence on the political plane has its complement in Franciscan poverty. Does not Franciscan poverty announce in an intemperate manner - out of season certainly with respect to every reasonable and ordered economy - the end of the curse which is attached to the private and selfish appropriation of goods? Doesn't a wide and generous vision of the redemption teach us to read some signs of the Kingdom to come in the most absurd endeavors connected with the destruction of the Monster of capitalism and the Leviathan of the State? □ PAUL RICOEUR

Religion is to be defended not by putting to death, but by dying; not by cruelty but by patient endurance; not by crime but by faith. If you wish to defend religion by bloodshed, you no longer defend it but pollute and profane it. □ LACTANTIUS

And yet Cardinal Newman wrote once that not even to save the world, or to save good women and little children, could a single venial sin be committed. I spoke of this to Judith Beck, talking of means and ends, and she reminded me of the Tolstoy tales, The Godfather, and What Men Live By. Tolstoy is always, in these short and wonderful stories, reminding us that God sees all, can remedy all, can protect all, and so we can well trust also that if we forego

atomic weapons, taking the risk, God will prevent world
disaster. It will not be a Communism that will prevail, but
we who believe. All things are possible to those who believe.
"Lord, I believe, help Thou my unbelief."

. . . Certainly when [I] lie in jail thinking of these
things, thinking of war and peace, and the problems of
human freedom . . . and the apathy of great masses of
people who believe that nothing can be done, I am all the
more confirmed in my faith in the little way of St. Therese.
We do the minute things that come to hand, we pray our
prayers, and beg also for an increase of faith — and God
will do the rest.

> [Written during a thirty-day sentence which
> she and three other Catholic Workers (Ammon
> Hennacy, Deane Mowrer, and Kerran
> Duggan) served for willful defiance of New
> York's 1957 Civil Defense Drills. Judith Beck
> was a young actress who had joined the Work-
> ers in their civil disobedience, carrying a sign
> which read, "Love and Life, Not Death and
> Taxes."]

By now it was after twelve and the room was cold and the
windows rattling in the wind . . . I got up and put on
sweater and scarf, and propping myself up in bed, began to
read what was at hand . . . I had gone through the Mass
for the next day, and turned to the February volume of
Butler's Lives of the Saints . . . There were Sts. Romanus
and Lupicinus, the former beginning as a hermit, but soon
joined, as hermits are, by others. First by his brother

Lupicinus, then by his sister, so that monasteries and convents grew up in the forests of the Jura mountains between France and Switzerland. I had read about these mountains before in The Path to Rome, of Hilaire Belloc (a wonderful book to read on a pilgrimage) and also in the memoirs of Kropotkin who had learned his anarchism from the watchmakers, villagers of the Jura mountains. The Little Flower's father also learned watchmaking there. They led a simple life, these monks of 470 A.D., but the account tells us that after imitating the fathers of the desert, they had been enriched by many gifts and changed their diet, which was only bread, made of barley and bran and pulse, often without salt or oil, and began to bring to table wheaten bread, fish, and other food. But Lupicinus was the most austere of them all. He slept in an old tree trunk and ate only dry bread moistened in cold water.

I can only say [in response to charges of communist sympathy and general troublemaking] "I am a daughter of the Church," repeating the words of St. Teresa of Avila. It is as a daughter of the Church that I do these things. I might add as a working journalist also and the two are not in opposition, muddied as our motives often are.

The Cross, the Cross
Goes deeper in than we know,
Deeper into life;
Right to the marrow
And through the bone.
□ D.H. LAWRENCE

The Cross does not preach to the Christian the passive endurance of injustice with no corresponding effort to uproot injustice; though it insists that only in the doing to death of self, in turning the other cheek to affronts to the self, is injustice to be overcome. Suffering, humiliation, and death -spiritual and physical- are not merely rewarded by "pie in the sky," but are the means to work here and now for the regeneration of individuals and societies. □ FR. VICTOR WHITE, O.P.

The psychological accompaniments of the present war — above all, the incredible brutalization of common judgement, the mutual slanderings, the unprecedented fury of destruction, the unheard-of lying, and the inability of men to call a halt to the bloody demon — are uniquely fitted to force upon the attention of every thinking person the problem of the chaotic unconscious which slumbers uneasily beneath the ordered world of consciousness. This war has pitilessly revealed to civilized man that he is still a barbarian, and has at the same time shown what an iron scourge lies in store for him if ever again he should be tempted to make his neighbor responsible for his own evil qualities. The psychology of the individual is reflected in the psychology of the nation. What the nation does is done also by each individual, and so long as the individual continues to do it, the nation will do likewise. Only a change in the attitude of the individual can initiate a change in the psychology of the nation. The great problems of humanity were never yet solved by general laws, but only through the regeneration of the attitudes of individuals. If ever there was a time when self reflection was the absolutely necessary and only right thing, it is now, in our present catastrophic epoch. Yet whoever reflects upon himself is bound to strike upon the frontiers of the unconscious, which contains all he needs to know. □ C.G. JUNG

Before all, money! Gold! For this barbarous god that has shed, and continues to shed, so much human blood, we have scourged ourselves and still scourge ourselves. We fight wars; on both sides we scourge ourselves on account of money! Two capitalisms confront each other and struggle for a morsel in the name of freedom and democracy . . . From now on we can destroy all life on earth and blow up the planet itself. We can employ frightful new means of creating misery; we have not given them up and we are certainly not going to. Are we drunk? Are we insane? The First World War killed ten million people; the second, forty million; the third, should it occur, has every prospect of far exceeding a hundred million. One can truly say that the Devil leads the dance . . . God did not create the world to make Hell on earth. God did not create man that he might be a perpetual murderer. □ CARDINAL SALIEGE, ARCHBISHOP OF TOULOUSE.

Since reaching manhood, I have encountered in history many conquerors whose face I found hideous, because I read there hatred and solitude. You see, they were nothing if they could not be conquerors. Their very existence depended on killing and enslaving. But there is another race of men who help us to breathe, who have never known existence and freedom except in the freedom and happiness of all and who consequently find reason to live and to love in defeat itself. Such men will never be alone. □ ALBERT CAMUS

If these hours be dark, as indeed in many ways they are, at least do not let us sit deedless, like fools and fine gentlemen, thinking the common toil not good enough for us, and beaten by the muddle; but rather let us work like good fellows trying by some dim candelight to set our workshop ready against tomorrow's daylight, that tomorrow when the civilized world, no longer greedy, strifeful, and destructive, shall have a new art, a glorious art, made by the People and for the People as a happiness to the maker and the user. □ WILLIAM MORRIS

Capitalism is as far removed from Christianity as Communism itself. □ ARCHBISHOP JUAN LANDAZURI OF LIMA, PERU

The way is shown by God in his "direction," the Torah. This God directs, that is, He teaches us to distinguish between the true way and the false ways. His direction, His teaching of the distinction, is given to us. But it is not enough to accept it. We must "delight" in it, we must cling to it with passion more exalted than all the passions of the wicked. Nor is it enough to learn it passively. We must again and again "mutter" it, we must repeat its living word after it, with our speaking we must enter into the word's spokenness so that it is spoken anew by us in our biological situation of today — and so on and on in eternal actuality. He who in his own activity serves the God Who reveals Himself — even though he may be sprung from a mean, earthly realm — is transplanted by the streams of water of the Direction. Only now can his own being thrive, ripen and bring forth fruit, and the law by which seasons of greenness and seasons of withering succeed one another in the life of the living being, no longer holds for him — his sap circulates continually in undiminished freshness. ☐ MARTIN BUBER

One of the researches most urgently needed is into the whole problem of compromise and noncompromise. I am dangerously and mistakenly much against compromise: "my kind never gets anything done." The (self-styled) "Realists" are quite as dangerously ready to compromise. They seem never sufficiently aware of the danger: they much too quickly and easily respect the compromise and come at rest in it. I would suppose that nothing is necessarily wrong with compromise of itself, except that those who are easy enough to make it are easy enough to relax into it and accept it, and that it thus inevitably becomes fatal. Or more nearly, the essence of the trouble is that compromise is held to be virtue of itself. ☐ JAMES AGEE

There is real and genuine tolerance only when a man is firmly and absolutely convinced of a truth or of what he holds to be a truth and when he at the same time recognizes the right of those who deny this truth to exist and to contradict him and to speak their own mind, not because they are free from truth but because they seek truth in their own way, and because he respects in them human nature and human dignity and those very resources of intellect and of conscience which make them potentially capable of attaining the truth he loves, if some day they happen to see it. ☐ JACQUES MARITAIN

Worship is the radical and deliberate cult of revolution . . . The will which has met its God confronts the world with new tables of the law . . . An honest religion is thus the natural ally of an honest revolution. □ WILLIAM ERNEST HOCKING

What is the meaning of poverty within the Church? No one can deny that it was chosen by the incarnate Son of God, Who being rich, made Himself poor. This choice He constantly maintained throughout His life, from the stable at Bethlehem to the nudity of the Cross. What is more, He preached poverty and held it forth as an inescapable demand for those who wished to be His disciples.

This seems to me to constitute above all the mystery of poverty in the Church; a mystery, moreover, which is bound up not only with its evangelical origins but its entire history. So much so that the great epochs, the great movements of internal reformation and renewal within the Church, and the periods of its most auspicious expansion throughout the world have invariably been those epochs in which the spirit of poverty has been affirmed and lived to the most manifest degree. □ GIACOMO CARDINAL LERCARO, ARCHBISHOP OF BOLOGNA

My mother used to say that the best cure for melancholy was to clean house, take a bath, get dressed up and go buy a new hat. St. Teresa of Avila is supposed to have fed her nuns steak when they were weakened by melancholy. My cure in this case was Dickens. I reread "David

Copperfield." My confusion of mind [she had come down with the flu] might have been increased by reading Charles Williams's "The Greater Trumps," but there was a splendid quotation which helped me greatly:

". . . When her brother had remarked that she seemed mopey she had been shocked . . . by a sense of her own disloyalty since she believed enjoyment to be a debt which every man owes to his fellows, partly for its own sake, partly lest he at all diminish their own precarious hold on it. She attempted dutifully to enjoy and failed, but while she attempted it the true gift was delivered into her hands." Joy in this sense is used as C.S. Lewis uses it in "Surprised by Joy," and as Bernanos meant it in his novel "Joy."

The man of religious faith must have a truer and more effective love for all men, including those who are our enemies. This is what the Church must do in a society where welfare is a secular project, achieved by machine-like organizations moving on the plane of science rather than love. The Church must bring out the ancient truth that every man is his brother's keeper and that it is not enough to refer him to a social agency. Charity today means condescending, heartless giving in order to be free of the sight of misery. Aid so given produces hatred and the recipient is not so much helped as humiliated. ☐ GUSTAVE WEIGEL, S.J.

This latest issue of Worship has an article on Confirmation which should be reprinted and given for study to every parent. There was a quotation which I copied in my diary which filled me with hope and joy.

"We must never forget that grace follows its own laws — different from those of natural psychology; and that even in natural life, spiritual maturity does not coincide with physical maturity. As St. Thomas says, it would be a dangerous materialization of grace to submit the Holy Spirit to the laws of the body. Child saints are the most beautiful proof of this." The article is by Boniface Luykx.

It is particularly necessary to maintain permanent and loving contact with every category of person, beginning with the most humble, the laborers, favoring among these the most ignorant, abandoned, needy, and unemployed . . . and exercising at the same time assiduous charity among the infirm, prisoners, and the like. □
POPE JOHN XXIII

The first duty of everyone is to become acutely conscious of the seriousness of the moral evil that unemployment constitutes for workers' homes. Moral evil, we say, and not a simple economic fact as alleged by certain economists' theories, which would not hesitate to propose it as a useful and even charitable solution in certain circumstances to facilitate recovery . . .

A moral evil because it strikes, through its burden of suffering, human beings in their heart . . . bringing insecurity, anguish for the next day, and often misery . . .

A *moral* evil because it violates the pattern of God, who wants man to work and be able to find, in the fruits of his labor, for himself and those dear to him, the means of living a human life. In a human economy, in a juster and better organized society, there must no longer be room for unemployment . . .

In a period of economic difficulties, firing is too easy a solution . . . If sacrifices are necessary, it is not the worker's wages which must be sacrificed first: it is the profits. □ ACHILLE CARDINAL LIENHART, BISHOP OF LILLE, *and* EMILE MAURICE GUERRY, ARCH-BISHOP OF CAMBRAI [*on the firing of 527 employees by the Fives-Lillie-Cail Co. In Lille*]

The commandment of love is the final law of the universe, although everything in nature and in man seems to disprove it. Love is the sole law which should govern the moral world. It is a doctrine difficult to believe, as the law is difficult to practice; but the law is final. It is the last word that has been uttered by Divine and human philosophy. □ CANON P.A. SHEEHAN

From St. Paul (2 Cor 14) to St. Basil; from St. Basil to St. Thomas of Aquin; and from St. Thomas to Pope Leo XIII, the Christian teaching has been that superfluous goods are a trust to be administered for the benefit of the needy. □ JOHN A. RYAN

The bourgeois mind is optimistic; it believes in the natural harmony of contradictory interests. Socialists, in the wide sense of the word, seem to be pessimistic, because our social reality appears to them to be wicked — and in that respect they are much nearer to the Christian mind than are the bourgeois. □ NICHOLAS BERDYAEV

To wrest from Nature is WORK.
To wrest from those who wrest from Nature is TRADE.
To wrest from those who wrest from those who wrest from Nature is FINANCE.
□ VINCENT McNABB, O.P.

I respect only poverty and great adventures of the mind; between the two there is only a society which is laughable. □ ALBERT CAMUS

As Socialists, we want a socialist world not because we have the conceit that men would therefore be happy . . . but because we feel the moral imperative in life itself to raise the human condition, even if this should ultimately mean no more than that man's suffering has been lifted to a higher level. □ NORMAN MAILER

I feel that all families should have the conveniences and comforts which modern living brings and which do simplify life, and give time to read, to study, to think, and to pray. And to work in the apostolate, too. But poverty is my vocation, to live as simply and poorly as I can, and never to

cease talking and writing of poverty and destitution. Here and everywhere. "While there are poor, I am of them. While men are in prison, I am not free," as Debs said and as we often quote.

Whatever attempts there may have been in the past to justify war, or at least to recognize a certain spiritual value in war, we ought to proclaim as loudly as possible that war with the face it wears today is sin itself. □ GABRIEL MARCEL

By definition, a government has no conscience; sometimes it has a policy, but nothing more. □ ALBERT CAMUS

Would the great religious leaders have preferred to die themselves rather than sanction the use of a weapon that brought the gift of life under total jeopardy? Specifically what would Christ do? If this question is irrelevant, then nothing in Christianity is relevant to the human situation today! □ NORMAN COUSINS

All these new saints of ours — new Christians, and loving persons who crowd the slums, and rediscover Christ in themselves and in others — lack power to explain; they merely exist. Through them, or rather through the heart which they infuse, literature and intellect will return, art and mental vigor will be restored to us. It would seem that the bowels and viscera of society must be heated first, and thereafter in time — it may be a century or two — a warmer life will reach the mind. These new grubs that creep out of the ground, these golden bees that dart by us in the sunshine, going so directly to their work like camp nurses, are more perfect creatures than we are, in that they deal with humanity as a unit. You and I are nothing to them. They have a relation to the whole. They are living in a beam which we do not see, they are the servants of a great cure which we cannot give, and do not understand. ☐ JOHN JAY CHAPMAN

Poverty and persecution should not be actively sought after, but they are the logical consequence of total struggle against the existing system. ☐ CAMILO TORRES

Every genuine human encounter must be inspired by poverty of spirit. We must forget ourselves in order to let the other person approach us. We must be able to open up to him, to let his distinctive personality unfold — even though it often frightens or repels us. We often keep the other person down, and only see what we want to see; thus we never really encounter the mysterious secret of his being, only ourselves. Failing to risk the poverty of encounter, we indulge in a new form of self assertion and pay the price for it: loneliness. Because we did not risk the poverty of openness (cf. Matthew 10:39), our lives are not graced with the warm fullness of human existence. We are left with only a shadow of our real self. ☐ JOHANNES B. METZ

SAINT JEROME

Whether or not the poor man profits more from grace because he is poor, poverty is a state to be venerated as such, because it was Christ's state. This is a most mysterious truth. Whatever his spiritual dispositions, whether a given poor man is holy or otherwise, whether he is well or badly treated — look at him simply as poor, as lacking what he needs, as wretched, and by itself this has a sacramental value. Bossuet calls it "the mark of Jesus Christ" . . . He may bear this "mark of the voluntary self-abasement of God incarnate" with bitterness and rage. If so, he is turning it into the most tragic paradox; he does not want for himself something Christ wanted passionately, and which, therefore, all men are called at least to consent to. It makes no difference; it is still Christ who begs, Christ who suffers, Christ who, in him, needs everything, even if he, poor wretch, fails Christ.
☐ PIE-RAYMOND REGAMEY, O.P.

St. Jerome wrote, "Let sleep creep over you holding a book, and let the sacred page receive your drooping face. . . . Reading is the oil that keeps the lamp burning." With the guidance of a priest some of the young people in town have had scripture classes this last month. Abbe Bouyer's "Meaning of Scripture" is a wonderful introduction to the Bible. When I spoke at St. Anselm's, Mary Perkins Ryan gave me her latest translation of his work "Introduction to Spirituality" in page proofs and I am looking forward to reading that. Notre Dame University Press brings out his work . . .

Democracy, just as a political concept, is meaningless for any society larger than a small city or a rural commune. Our so-called democracies in the Western world are oligarchies subject more or less to periodical revision (which never changes their oligarchical structure), and in this they do not differ essentially from the oligarchies that rule the communist world. The people, in any human corporate sense, do not determine any policies outside their backyards. The world is governed by the representatives of industry, finance, technology, and by bureaucracies in the paid service of these powerful groups — governed, not in the interests of the people as a whole, not even of all the people in any one country, and not even nowadays for personal profit, but primarily for the self-satisfying exercise of power. □ SIR HERBERT READ

The duty of the Incarnation, if we were faithful to the meaning of the word, would oblige us to maintain simultaneously, at each moment of time, the most contradictory-to-good-sense positions; to die to the world, even while we committed ourselves to it: to deny the everyday, and to save it; to sorrow over our sins, and to rejoice in the new man; to reckon of value only what is inward, but to spread ourselves abroad throughout nature in order to conquer the whole of life for inwardness; to recognize in ourselves the dependence of a nothing and the liberty of a king: and above all, never to regard any of these divided situations as substantially contradictory, nor as finally resolvable in the experience of man. □ EMMANUEL MOUNIER

The main point in the contemplative life is looking at God and his truth, the thing all human existence is directed towards. So you have Augustine writing in The Trinity that "wondering appreciation of God is held out to us as our be-all and end-all, our everlasting cup of joy." When we see God face-to-face in the next life the cup will be full, for God will make us completely happy. The way we apprehend God now is imperfect, second-hand, paradoxical; all the same, the process does begin, and it will be brought to completion in the afterlife. Doesn't Aristotle's Ethics say a man's greatest happiness is staring at the highest intelligible being?

A study of the effects of God's work inevitably directs our attention to God Himself — the mysterious elements in God can be more readily grasped once the world, His creation, is understood (Romans 1:20). The contemplative life, then, has a second component: the investigation of nature, the world and whatever derives from God. Another way to come to know God! To quote Augustine once more, "when you set out to acquaint yourself with the natural wonders science disclosed, don't flit from one fact to another just to satisfy your curiosity, but carefully penetrate the various levels of reality until you come to the permanent and the eternal!"

So instead of loving what you think is peace, love other men and love God above all. And instead of hating the people you think are warmongers, hate the appetites and the disorder in our own soul, which are the causes of war. If you love peace, then hate injustice, hate tyranny, hate greed — but hate these things in yourself, not in another. ☐ EDGAR FORAND

There does not appear to have been any specifically Catholic reaction to the Profumo affair. Certain sections of Catholic opinion are, of course, always excited by public disclosures of sexual immorality and rush to account for them in terms of the falling away of society from religious practice. To be frank, those societies in which religion has a more important role than it has in modern Britain are not conspicuously successful in solving this particular problem. It is even true that the shrillness, the feverishness of some religious denunciations of sexual faults represent an ill-balanced view of sexuality and a refusal to accept it for what it is within the order of creation.

Most remarkable of all, there is the general disposition to get excited about fornication co-existing with a steady refusal to get excited about murder. Here I have in mind, not the relatively rare crime for which in this civilized country the penalty is that a man shall be hanged by the neck until he is dead, but the preparations for mass slaughter with nuclear weapons. Future historians, if there should be any, will marvel that in the years when the ICBMs were in a state of continual readiness to incinerate vast populations the greatest shock to the moral sensibility of the British people should have been a liason between a politician and a prostitute. ☐ J.M. CAMERON

We cannot wish men to be unhappy so that we may have a chance to show our mercy. You give bread to a poor man; it would be far better if none went hungry, and such help was not needed. Do away with misery and there will be no need for works of mercy. But will the glory of charity cease to exist because there are no more works of mercy? ☐ ST. AUGUSTINE

There can be no perfect virtue, none that bears fruit, unless it be exercised by means of our neighbor. □ CATHERINE OF SIENA

We begin by lacking charity towards Nature, so that instead of trying to co-operate with Tao or the Logos on the inanimate and sub-human levels, we try to dominate and exploit, we waste the earth's mineral resources, ruin its soil, ravage its forests, pour filth into its rivers and poisonous fumes into its air. From lovelessness in relation to Nature we advance to lovelessness in relation to art — a lovelessness so extreme that we have effectively killed all the fundamental or useful arts and set up various kinds of mass-production by machines in their place. And of course this lovelessness in regard to art is at the same time a lovelessness in regard to the human beings who have to perform the fool-proof and grace-proof tasks imposed by our mechanical art-surrogates and by the interminable paperwork connected with mass-production and mass-distribution. With mass-production and mass-distribution go mass-financing, and the three have conspired to expropriate ever-increasing numbers of small owners of land and productive equipment, thus reducing the sum of freedom among the majority and increasing the power of a minority to exercise a coercive control over the lives of their fellows. This coercive controlling minority is composed of private capitalists or government bureaucrats or of both classes of bosses acting in collaboration — and, of course, the coercive and therefore essentially loveless nature of the control remains the same, whether the bosses call themselves "company directors" or "civil servants." □ ALDOUS HUXLEY

And now Cardinal Spellman, God bless him, has added still another prayer to those at the conclusion of Masses in the New York archdiocese, the Divine Praises: Blessed be God, Blessed be His Holy Name . . . and so on, like a creed, a declaration of faith. It is indeed an invocation of the Name.

In regard to the Name, Abbe Louis Bouyer in The Meaning of Holy Scripture, (University of Notre Dame Press) has this to say:

> "It is the supreme expression of His presence (after the Angel, the Face, the Shekinah, His presence in the fire and the cloud) more spiritual and more personal than all the others."

Do we believe this, do we believe in the Holy Name and the power of the Holy Name? It was reading The Way of the Pilgrim, published by Harpers, and also included in Russian Spirituality by Fedotov, a collection of the writings of the Russian saints, that brought me first to a knowledge of what the Holy Name meant in our lives . . . Fordham Russian Center has a pamphlet, On the Invocation of the Name, which teaches us to pray without ceasing, with every breath we draw, with every beat of our hearts. And lastly, J.D. Salinger in the New Yorker, in his stories Frannie and Zooey, later published in book form, brings us again to a concept of the meaning of the Name.

With this recognition of the importance of the Word made flesh and dwelling among us, still with us in the bread and wine of the altar, how can any priest tear though the Mass as though it were a repetitious duty? . . . And some of the best priests I have met do this, abusing *the prayers of the Mass in this way.*

I am begging them not to.

". . . You cannot fail to see the power of mere words,"
Joseph Conrad wrote in his preface to A Personal Record.
"Such words as Glory, for instance, or Pity. Shouted with
perseverance, with ardour, with conviction, these two by
their sound alone have set whole nations in motion and up-
heaved the dry hard ground on which rests our whole social
fabric."

So I am praying that at the Council and at all the
Masses at the Council, the Word made flesh will be among
them. Forsake them not, O Lord, our God.

What is American Christianity; where does it take
root: is it not yet to come in its personal expression, its
image and its martyrdom? Faulkner has patiently
probed and plodded in seeming shadows to find this
vein; turning sometimes towards Catholicism in a quite
explicit way — his dynasties are always Scotch, not
Irish — as if visualizing a reconversion of Protest-
ants . . .

Step by step, the great writer leads us to a
rediscovery of Christ in modern times: one winces at
the vulgar and ignorant criticisms with which he has
been lynched, stigmatizing him as an obscene and rac-
ist writer, retaining just one phrase quoted probably
out of context, in abnormal circumstances, one violent
symbol of horror and castigation that can be equalled
by Euripides. Aeschylus or Dostoievsky, none of them
'nice writers', overlooking his love of man, not as a
race but an individual, his immense, labyrinthine soul-
searching that culminated in the great story that he
wryly called A Fable knowing too well that the modern

world, like the Grand Inquisitor would not recognize this parable of Christ and Peace. □ ANNE TAILLEFER *As Faulkner Lies Dead*

That man is a Catholic who opens himself to all and allows the universal love of the Lord to resound in his heart. He is a Catholic who, when he remembers the mercy of Christ towards him, becomes merciful, that is to say, overwhelmed by distress, whatever form that distress may take. He is a Catholic who instinctively rejects everything that is a source of division, who cannot meet anyone without tirelessly seeking out an area of agreement. He is a Catholic who sees in each man not the social category to which he belongs, nor the label which is applied to him, of unbeliever or Protestant or Jew or Communist, but the brother for whom Christ died and who has been placed in his path in order to receive his love. Finally, he is a Catholic who, through humility, has made himself poor in spirit and is always ready to welcome those who are deprived whether it be of material good or of the light of faith. □ MSGR. HUYGHE, BISHOP OF ARRAS.

From having all these and other like feelings I noted that interior prayer bears fruit in three ways: in the Spirit, in the feelings, and in revelations. In the first, for instance, is the sweetness of the love of God, inward peace, gladness of mind, purity of thought, and the sweet remembrance of God. In the second, the pleasant warmth of the heart, fullness of delight in all one's limbs, the joyous 'bubbling' in the heart, lightness and courage, the joy of living, power not to feel sickness and sorrow. And in the last, light given to the mind, understanding of Holy Scripture, knowledge of the speech of created things, freedom from fuss and vanity, knowledge of the joy of the inner life, and finally certainty of the nearness of God and of His love for us. □ THE WAY OF THE PILGRIM

By a thousand cunning attachments and controls, visible and subliminal, the workers in an expanding economy are tied to a consumption mechanism: they are assured of a livelihood provided they devour without undue selectivity all that is offered by the machine — and demand nothing that is not produced by the machine. The whole organization of the metropolitan economy is designed to kill spontaneity and self-direction. You stop on the red light and go on the green. You see what you are supposed to see, think what you are supposed to think: your personal contributions, like your income and security taxes, are deductible at source. To choose, to select, to discriminate, to exercise prudence, or continence, to carry self-control to the point of abstinence, to have standards other than those of the market, and to set limits other than those of immediate consumption — these are impious heresies that would challenge the whole megalapolitan myth and deflate its economy. In such a "free" society, Henry Thoreau must rank as a greater public enemy than Karl Marx.

The metropolis, in its final stage of development, becomes a collective contrivance for making this irrational system work, and for giving those who are in reality its victims the illusion of power, wealth, and felicity, of standing at the very pinnacle of human achievement. But in actual fact their lives are constantly in peril, their wealth is tasteless and ephemeral, their

St.Dorothy
martyr

leisure is sensationally monotonous, and their pathetic felicity is tainted by constant, well-justified anticipations of violence and sudden death. Increasingly they find themselves "strangers and afraid" in a world they never made: a world ever less responsive to direct human command, ever more empty of human meaning. □ LEWIS MUMFORD

Humility . . . is absolutely necessary if a man is to avoid acting like a baby all his life. To grow up means, in fact, to become humble, to throw away the illusion that I am the center of everything and that other people only exist to provide me with comfort and pleasure. Unfortunately, pride is so deeply embedded in human society that instead of educating one another for humility and maturity, we bring each other up in selfishness and pride. The attitudes that ought to make us "mature" too often only give us a kind of poise, a kind of veneer, that make our pride all the more suave and effective. For social life, in the end, is too often simply a convenient compromise by which your pride and mine are able to get along together without too much friction.

That is why it is a dangerous illusion to trust in society to make us balanced, realistic, and humble. Very often the humility demanded of us by our society is simply an acquiescence in the pride of the collectivity and of those in power. Worse still, while we learn to be humble and virtuous as individuals, we allow ourselves to commit the worst crimes in the name of "society". We are gentle in our private life in order to be murderers as a collective group. For murder, committed by an individual, is a great crime. But when it becomes war or revolution, it is represented as the summit of heroism and virtue. □ THOMAS MERTON

The reason why a good end cannot legitimate the evil means which appear necessary for its attainment is because, morally speaking, the two are unrelated. An intrinsically evil act can never produce directly a good effect. The emergence of good results from apparently unworthy antecedents is due to the operation of forces which are strictly proportioned to their effects but hidden from view under accompanying, though incidental, evils. Normally the attempt to excuse wrong actions on the grounds that they subserve a good end can be ascribed to mental confusion or malice. The relation which is imagined to exist between ends and means does not in fact exist at all, or has been arbitrarily imposed by the mind. The realities of the case have been ignored and the situation falsified. Thus there can be no relation of means to ends between the bombing and wholesale destruction of innocent people and the maintenance in being of the Catholic Church, between tyrannical forms of government and the happiness and good estate of the community at large, between aggressive nationalism and the general peace of the world. □ DOM AELRED GRAHAM

The meeting [of the Pentecostal movement] was an amazing coming together of 16,500 people at Atlantic City. Always I distrusted crowds, mass enthusiasm. Peter Maurin once gave us a book to read called The Devil's Share, by de Rougemont, which told of mass movements, and people's desire to be swayed, influenced, "beside themselves," swept by a common joy as in a football game or a baseball game. Mobs, lynching mobs, too, feel this singleness of purpose. Something takes possession of them at such times, de Rougemont points out. Father Ronald Knox wrote a book called Enthusiasm years ago, about mass movements in the Church, and many Catholics thought the Catholic Worker movement was tarred with that brush.

Hilaire Belloc begins one of his essays with whimsical irony by relating how he started a speech in this way: POVERTY.

1. The attainment of it.
2. The retention of it when attained.

It appears that no one was interested and soon he was addressing a vacant hall. St. Francis loved poverty, and with the courtesy of a troubadour regarded Lady Poverty as his lovely mistress. And Leon Bloy, who lived a long life with her, speaks thus: "The angels are silent, and the trembling Devils tear out their tongues rather than speak. Only the idiots of our own genera- tion have taken upon themselves to elucidate this mystery. Meanwhile, till the deep shall swallow them up, Poverty walks tranquilly in her mask, bearing her sieve." □ WILLIAM GAUCHAT

When we were growing up, we were taught that it was in bad taste to talk about money, and yet one finds Anthony Trollope's and Jane Austen's characters constantly talking about income. "Aunt Greenow has a fortune of 40,000 pounds" and "poor Kate's fortune is less than 100 pounds a year!"

We may not look at pleasure to go to heaven in featherbeds. It is not the way; for Our Lord Himself went thither with great pain and by many tribulations. □ ST. THOMAS MORE

May the power of your love, O Lord, fiery and sweet as honey, wean my heart from all that is under heaven, so that I may die for love of your love, You Who were so good as to die for love of my love. □ ST. FRANCIS OF ASSISI

The price we have to pay for money is paid in liberty. And there are many luxuries that we may legitimately prefer to it, such as a grateful conscience, or the [pursuit] of our inclinations. Trite, flat, and obvious as this conclusion may appear, we have only to look around us in society to see how scantily it has been recognized; and perhaps even ourselves, after a little reflection, may decide to spend a trifle less for money and indulge ourselves a trifle more in the article of freedom . . . It is true that we might do a vast amount of good if we were wealthy, but it is also highly improbable; not many do; and the art of growing rich is not only quite distinct from that of doing good, but the practice of the one does not at all train a man for practicing the other. □ ROBERT LOUIS STEVENSON

If we kill men, what brothers will we have left? With whom shall we live then? □ NHAT HANH

St. Remigius, Bishop of Rheims, needed, due to his high office and duties, a more spacious dwelling than a member of his flock, but when he saw his palace burn to the ground his comment was indicative of his attachment to it. "A fire," he said, "is always a pleasant sight." □ WILLIAM GAUCHAT

Whatever the program, for whatever purpose or cause, if love is not there, then beware. Without love there can be temporary successes but with time they crumble. □ POPE JOHN XXIII

From the beginning, My Church has been what it is today, and will be until the end of time, a scandal to the strong, a disappointment to the weak, the ordeal and the consolation of those interior souls who seek in it nothing but Myself. Yes . . . whoever looks for Me there will find Me there; but he will have to look, and I am better hidden than people think, or than certain of My priests would have you believe. I am still more difficult to discover than I was in the little stable at Bethlehem for those who will not approach Me humbly, in the footsteps of the shepherds and the Magi. It is true that palaces have been built in My honor, with galleries and peristyles without number, magnificently illuminated day and night, populated with guards and sentries. But if you want to find Me there, the clever thing is to do as they did on the old road in Judaea, buried under the snow, and ask for the only thing you need - a star and a pure heart. □ GEORGES BERNANOS

We must do everything we are obliged to do: give without reckoning, practice virtue whenever opportunity offers, constantly overcome ourselves, prove our love by all the little acts of tenderness and consideration we can muster. In a word, we must produce all the good works that lie within our strength — out of love for God. But it is in truth indispensible to place our whole trust in Him Who alone sanctifies our works and Who can sanctify us without works for He can even raise children to Abraham out of stones. Yes, it is needful, when we have done everything that we believe we have to do, to confess ourselves unprofitable servants, at the same time hoping that God out of grace will give us everything we need. This is the little way of childhood. ☐ ST. THERESE OF LISIEUX

My personal definition of voluntary poverty is this: the sincere will to do without as much as one can in order to be free to live a full human life. ☐ WILLIAM GAUCHAT

Seeking safety from occasional robbers, those who are recognized as robbers, we fall into the hands of permanent robbers, the organized ones, those who are recognized as benefactors; we fall into the hands of governments. ☐ LEO TOLSTOY

As I see it, the death penalty is in itself a sin of homicide committed by society. ☐ JACQUES MARITAIN

Go to the political world; see nation jealous of nation, trade rivalling trade, armies and fleets matched against each other. Survey the various ranks of the community, its parties and their contests, the strivings of the ambitious, the intrigues of the crafty. What is the end of all this turmoil? The grave. What is the measure? The cross. □ CARDINAL NEWMAN

What does it matter to us," answer the politicians, "what can it matter to us . . . We have unlearnt the Republic but we have learnt how to govern. See the elections. They are admirable. They will improve. They will become all the better, since it is we who make them. And since we are beginning to know how to make them." The government makes the elections, the elections make the government . . . The government makes the deputies, the deputies make the government. All oblige. The populations look on. The country is requested to pay . . . This is not a vicious circle as you might believe. It is not in the least vicious. It is a circle, just that, a closed circuit, a closed circle. All circles are closed. Otherwise they would not be circles. This is not quite what our founders had foreseen . . . Founders come first. Profiteers come after. □ CHARLES PEGUY

Our Maggie [from Tivoli] when she was saving money towards settling in West Virginia, had a job in a neighboring village from eleven at night until seven in the morning, on an assembly line where a few motions glued a Timex watch box together, which box is discarded of course as soon as the watch is taken out. Small factory work in the country would not be so bad if something useful were being turned out. But what a torture to do such useless work! I am reminded of the words of Dostoevsky, in The House of the Dead (his Siberian prison experience):

"The idea has occurred to me that if one wanted to crush, to annihilate a man utterly, to inflict on him the most terrible of punishments so that the most ferocious murderer would shudder at it and dread it beforehand, one need only give him work of absolutely, completely useless and irrational character. Though the hard labor now enforced is uninteresting and wearisome for the prisoner, yet in itself as work it is rational: the convict makes bricks, digs, does plastering, building; there is sense and meaning in such work. The convict worker sometimes grows keen over it, tries to work more skillfully, faster, better. But if he had to pour water from one vessel into another and back, over and over again, to pound sand, to move a heap of earth from one place to another and back again — I believe the convict would hang himself in a few days or would commit a thousand crimes, preferring to die rather than to endure such humiliation, shame and torture. Of course such punishment would become a torture, a form of vengeance, and would be senseless, as it would achieve no rational object. But such torture, senselessness, humiliation, and shame is an inevitable element in all forced labor; penal labor is incomparably more painful than any other free labor — just because it is forced."

During Sunday I read the life of Mother Seton. The first years of her work in founding the Sisters of Charity in America held much hardship for her little community. The sisters subsisted on carrot-coffee, salt pork and butter milk during one winter. For Christmas they had smoked sardines . . . and it was so cold a winter that they had to sweep the snow out of their rooms which had drifted through the crevices by the barrelful!

In the whole world, Christ suffers dismemberment . . . His Mystical Body is drawn and quartered from age to age . . . As long as we are on earth the love that unites us will bring us suffering by our very contact with one another, because this love is the resetting of a Body of broken bones. ☐ THOMAS MERTON

We must be saved together. We must come to God together. Together we must all return to our Father's house. What would God say to us if some of us came to Him without the others? ☐ CHARLES PEGUY

To love is not to experience a particular sensation in the heart; that emotion is but a reflex phenomenon, a detail of love at the least. To love is to wish for the good, it is to give the best of one's self for the good of another; it does not mean grasping for one's self; love means giving one's self.

As long as the understanding finds no trouble or difficulty and is at ease, that is a sign that one's faith has not gone far enough. ☐ MAURICE LANDRIEUX

THE PRISONER

Thy servant is in irons
In the shadow of death
Lord deliver him
I see his face behind bars
Like a saint's face in holy pictures
His wide face protruding eyes
Fringe of black hair on his brow
Streaked with white wool
He looks like the Christ
Of Quentin Matsys
He gazes straight in front
Stunned at his misfortune
He sees God's sky
And that all will go well
No he is not yet painted
In the holy pictures
He sits on his bed
His head in his arms
He weeps
Alone among enemies
Who hate all he loves
For whom his kindness his intelligence
Are objects of contempt
Prisoner of his innocence
He keeps patience
Like his Master Jesus Christ
Like Him sorrowful unto death
He has so loved Justice
He is like the Christ
Of Quentin Matsys
He is learning the language of heaven.
□ RAISSA MARITAIN

When we enter upon the duties of any office, as that of regent, preacher, or superior, we ought to prepare ourselves for it by some practice of humility, mortification, or charity such as visiting prisoners or the poor in hospitals, serving in the kitchen, etc . . .

We must hope and expect great things from God, because the merits of Our Lord belong to us; and to hope much in God is to honor Him much. The more we hope, the more we honor Him. ☐ FATHER LALLEMANT

Every good impulse, every noble deed we perform is of God, Christ in us. At the very same time there is an evil, complacent nagging going on, trying to discourage us, trying to impugn our motives, trying to spoil everything of good we do. This complacency, self-satisfaction, is to be scorned and silenced. It shows pride even to be surprised and grieved at the baseness, like sediment, at the bottom of every good deed. As long as we live there will be war, a conflict between nature and grace, nature again and again getting the upper hand for the moment, only to be put down rigidly. If we have faith and hope it is impossible to be discouraged.

If recollection seems difficult, at least accustom yourself to pronounce with your lips words which relate to the Passion; the habit of the lips easily becomes a habit of the heart, and within the cold heart the fire will gradually become warmer. ☐ ST. ANGELA OF FOLIGNA.

You never enjoy the world aright till the sea itself floweth in your veins, till you are clothed with the heavens and crowned with the stars; and perceive yourself to be sole heir of the whole world and more so because men are in it who are everyone sole heirs as well as you. Till you can sing and rejoice and delight in God, as misers do in gold, and kings in sceptres -you never can enjoy the world. □ THE MEDITATION OF TRAHERNE

Grace is sometimes compared to a fountain of living water, and again to a glowing fire . . . Divine grace, like water, purifies, refreshes, vivifies . . . What the soul does for the body, grace does for the soul. □ MAURICE LANDRIEUX

No efforts or expenses seem too great to purchase our escape from the afflictions which God sends us; and yet they are even more beneficial and more meritorious than voluntary penances. For God knows better than we in what regards and by what means our soul has need for being purified and regenerated. Besides, labours and penances which are taken on voluntarily and by choice leave still open, good as they are, a free field for self love. But those which come upon us unexpectedly and undesired, even if we endure them with patience or with joy, seem always impositions, not the growth of our own will and desire; and therefore they exclude pride, self-love and vanity. □ ST. ANGELA OF FOLIGNA

Many will never arrive at a high perfection, because they do not hope sufficiently. We must have a strong and solid hope, grounded on the mercy and infinite goodness of God, and on the infinite merits of Jesus Christ. □ FATHER LALLEMANT

There is only one unhappiness, and that is not to be one of the Saints. □ LEON BLOY

Community life brings into being a microcosm of the Church; on a small scale it gives an image of the whole reality of the Church. Thus the humble sign of community can have effects which far transcend the limitations of its members. Much more than ideas, the world of today needs images. No idea could possibly gain credit, unless supported by a visible reality; otherwise it would only be an ideology. Any sign, however weak, gains value in that it is a living reality. □ ROGER SCHUTZ

If anyone thinks that Christians regard unchastity as *the* great vice, he is quite wrong. The sins of the flesh are bad, but they are the least bad of all sins. All the worst pleasures are purely spiritual: the pleasure of putting other people in the wrong, of bossing and patronizing and spoiling sport, and back-biting; the pleasures of power, of hatred. □ C. S. LEWIS

There is no love without the cross, and no cross without a victim. And whether we be on the cross or beneath it weeping, there is Christ, and sorrow shall be turned to joy. □ WILLIAM GAUCHAT

When a son of a friend of ours took his own life years ago, I asked the Spanish priest at Our Lady of Guadalupe Church on 14th St. "Did he die in mortal sin?" I was remembering Kirilov in The Possessed by Dostoyevsky. The priest said, "There is no time with God, and all the prayers and Masses said for him after his death will have given him that moment of turning to God in penitence."

Never feel above an honorable calling, nor be afraid of the coarse frock or apron. Put your hands to work in the line of duty; dust on your garments and moisture on your brow neither shame nor disgrace. Better soil your hands than your character. □ DANIEL ORCUTT *Member of the early Shaker Community*

We do not suggest a denial of science and complicated technology, but a reordering, showing what is secondary . . . often dangerous, sometimes deadly, usually very costly, and finally, inadequate to resolve the great problems of the world: hunger, misery, slavery and war.

It seems to us that only simple and poor means can help in the establishment on this earth of the kingdom wished by God. The kingdom must be available to the poorest and realizable as soon as the necessary conversion of heart and spirit takes place. □ PIERRE PARODI

We must love them both, those whose opinions we share and those whose opinions we reject. For both have labored in the search for truth, and both have helped us in finding it. □ ST. THOMAS AQUINAS

Once we begin not to worry about what kind of house we are living in, what kind of clothes we are wearing, once we give up the stupid recreation of the world; we have time-which is priceless - to remember that we are our brothers' keepers and that we must not only care for his needs as far as we are immediately able, but we must try to build a better world.

What a fine place this world would be if Roman Catholics tried to keep up with St. Francis of Assisi. □ PETER MAURIN

Poverty signifies completeness without superfluity, wholeness without luxury: A state of holiness. □ ERIC GILL

All of a sudden I perceived that the silence was a presence. At the heart of the silence there was He Who is all stillness, all peace, all poise. □ GEORGES BERNANOS

It is this earthy spirituality that Christians need to recover if the Church is to be prophetic, wild and holy, and not merely socially enlightened . . . it is time to take the lid once more off the well of truth from which the mystics and saints drew. □ ROSEMARY HAUGHTON

The true liberal Catholic thinker recognizes that though the Church is founded on a rock, men build thereon 'gold, silver, precious stones, wood, hay, stubble.' From time to time an examination has to be made not of the foundation 'which is Christ Jesus' but of the lower courses of masonry laid down by man. □ VINCENT McNABB

Compassion is the chief law of human existence. □ FEODOR DOSTOEVSKY

I repeat: to know how to say the Our Father, and to know how to put it into practice, this is the perfection of the Christian life. POPE JOHN XXIII

Only men who create an interior unity in themselves, only men whose vision is global, whose heart is universal, will be valid instruments for the miracle of being violent as the prophets were violent, true as Christ was true, revolutionary as the gospel is revolutionary, without injuring love. □ DOM HELDER CAMARA

I have not the courage to search through books for beautiful prayers. . . . Unable either to say them all or choose between them, I do as a child would do who cannot read — I say just what I want to say to God, quite simply, and He never fails to understand.
□ ST. THERESE OF LISIEUX

The problem of evolution has never bothered me, nor the exact time when 'God breathed into man a living soul'. It was the observation of these beauties along the sea shore that brought me to a stunned recognition of God as creator of infinite beauty and variety.

St. Teresa of Avila said that she was so grateful a person that she could be bought with a sardine. It sounds obscure but I know what she meant. A man on the Bowery who presses a dollar into your hand . . . means so much to you that your heart swells with gratitude. And how much more for our readers all over the country who keep things going with large gifts and small.

We need to feast on beauty to refresh ourselves and to remember Dostoievsky's wonderful words "The world will be saved by beauty."

The good that men do is always in the realm of the uncertain and of the fluid, because the needs and sufferings of men, the sins and failures of men, are constant, and love triumphs, at least in this life, not by eliminating evil once for all but by resisting and overcoming it anew every day. The good is not assured once for all by one heroic act. It must be recaptured over and over again. St. Peter looked for a limit to forgiveness. Seven times, and then the sin was irreversible! But Christ told him that forgiveness must be repeated over and over again, without end. □ THOMAS MERTON

We certainly can try to grow in love, and it is good practice, this giving what we've got, whether it is a cup of coffee or money to pay the grocery bill. We ask you in the name of St. Therese, on whose feast I write, and in the name of St. Francis, whose feast comes tomorrow. It is always a feast where love is, and where love is, God is.

It was when he trusted his own strength that the Apostle succumbed to the jeers of a servant girl. When he relied upon his Lord he was able to defy an empire. And we are still living upon his victory. □ MAURICE ZUNDEL

THE SOWER

We are called to be saints, St. Paul said, and Peter Maurin called on us to make that kind of society where it was easier for men to be saints. Nothing less will work. Nothing less is powerful enough to combat war and the all-encroaching state.

To be a saint is to be a lover, ready to leave, to give all. Dostoievsky said that love in practice is a harsh and dreadful thing compared to love in dreams, but if 'we see only Jesus' in all who come to us . . . then it is easier. Father Faber says we are progressing if we begin over again each day in these resolutions.

In spite of the nuclear age we are living in, we can plant our gardens even if they are only window boxes, we can awaken ourselves to God's good earth and in little ways start going out on pilgrimage, to the suburbs, to the country, and when we get the grace, we may so put off the old man, and put on Christ, that we will begin to do without all that the City of Man offers us, and build up the farming commune, the Village, the City of God wherein justice dwelleth.

The rebel undoubtedly demands a certain degree of freedom for himself; but in no case, if he is consistent, does he demand the right to destroy the existence and the freedom of others. He humiliates no one. The freedom he claims, he claims for all . . . □ ALBERT CAMUS

There are times in our lives when we feel life flow in our veins, feel ourselves to be alive, we can look into our hearts and find there the Holy Trinity, the indwelling of the Holy Spirit. But we need to be alone, we need to have time, to be at rest, to be rested too . . . We need to sleep, we need to lose consciousness, to die in this way, in order to live-and this is on the natural plane. But grace builds on nature, and we must live in order to lead the supernatural life to its fullest.

Baron Von Hugel used to say that every morning as he made his plans for the day, he used to draw up a schedule of work to be done, and then cut half of it out. I should do the same about reading-draw up a list of books to be read, and then cut half of them out.

For fasting was ever the food of virtue. From abstinence there arise chaste thoughts, just decisions, salutary counsels. And through voluntary suffering the flesh dies to the concupiscences, and the spirit waxes strong in virtue. But as the salvation of our souls is not gained solely by fasting let us fill up what is wanting in our fasting with almsgiving to the poor. Let us give to virtue what we take from pleasure. Let the abstinence of the man who fasts be the dinner for the poor man. ☐ POPE ST. LEO

The key to the whole of life is to be able to put oneself in the second place. ☐ TURGENEV

Imagine the devil in the process of buying an unfortunate person's soul. Someone takes pity on the victim, intervenes in the debate and says to the devil: It is shameful to offer such a small price; the thing is worth twice as much. This sinister farce is the role the worker movement is playing, with its unions, parties and leftist intellectuals. □ SIMONE WEIL

Who does not know that kings and rulers took their beginnings from those who, being ignorant of God, have assumed, because of blind greed and intolerable presumption, to make themselves masters of their equals, namely men, by means of pride, violence, bad faith, murder, and nearly every kind of crime, being incited thereto by the prince of this world. The Devil? □ POPE GREGORY VII

We often hear of Jesus of Nazareth as a wandering teacher; and there is a vital truth in that view so far as it emphasizes an attitude towards luxury and convention which most respectable people would regard as that of a vagabond . . . It is well to speak of his wanderings in this sense that he shared the drifting life of the most homeless and the most hopeless of the poor. It is assuredly well to remember that he would quite certainly have been moved on by the police and almost certainly arrested by the police, for having no visible means of subsistence. For our law has in it a turn of humour or touch of fancy which Nero or Herod never happened to think of: that of actually punishing homeless people for not sleeping at home. □ G.K. CHESTERTON

Let our first act every morning be the following resolve: 'I shall not fear anyone on earth. I shall fear only God. I shall bear ill-will towards no one. I shall not submit to injustice from anyone.

I shall conquer truth and in resisting untruth I shall put up with all suffering.' □ MOHANDAS K. GANDHI

A genuine revolution of values means in the final analysis that our loyalties must become ecumenical rather than sectional. Every nation must now develop an overriding loyalty to mankind as a whole in order to preserve the best in their individual societies. □ MARTIN LUTHER KING

Of poverty - the affliction which actually or potentially includes all other afflictions - I would not dare to speak as from myself: and those who reject Christianity will not be moved by Christ's statement that poverty is blessed. But here a rather remarkable fact comes to my aid. Those who would most scornfully repudiate Christianity as a mere "Opiate of the people" have a contempt for the rich, that is, for all mankind *except* the poor. They regard the poor as the only people worth preserving from "liquidation", and place in them the only hope of the human race. But this is not compatible with a belief that the effects of poverty on those who suffer it are wholly evil; it even implies that they are good. The Marxist thus finds himself in real agreement with the Christian in those two beliefs which Christianity paradoxically demands - that poverty is blessed and yet ought to be removed. □ C.S. LEWIS

Greed is more than a virtue in the capitalist civilization; it is a cult. Men are taught it from early childhood in its various pleasing forms . . . Greed is not a nice word, and it is disguised under various fancy names, such as aggressiveness, shrewdness, holding your own, self-interest, and so on. □ W.E. WOODWARD

Only he who has measured the dominion of force, and knows how not to respect it, is capable of love and justice. □ SIMONE WEIL

If a man wishes to be sure of the road he treads on, he must close his eyes and walk in the dark. □ ST. JOHN OF THE CROSS

It is an evil thing to expect too much either from ourselves or from others. Disappointment in ourselves does not moderate our expectations from others; on the contrary, it raises them. It is as if we wished to be disappointed with our fellow men.

One does not really love mankind when one expects too much from them. □ ERIC HOFFER

If I knew the world were coming to an end tomorrow, I would still go out and plant my three apple trees today. □ MARTIN LUTHER

Now it is a terrible business to mark out a man for the vengeance of men. But it is a thing to which a man can grow accustomed . . . And the horrible thing about public officials, even the best . . . is not that they are wicked . . . not that they are stupid . . . it is simply that they have got used to it. □ G.K. CHESTERTON

The evil one is pleased with sadness and melancholy. □ ST. FRANCIS DE SALES

When has any man of prayer told us that prayer has failed him? □ GEORGES BERNANOS

I read my morning Psalms in the Anglican prayer book and hymnal which Ann Perkins gave me - it is so much easier to find one's way around in. The words "ordinary time" in our own prayer book put me in a state of confusion and irritation. To me, no times are "ordinary." C.S. Lewis did us all a great service in writing his book on the Psalms, a beautiful and most readable commentary. He is my favorite theologian.

No one in the world can alter truth. All we can do is seek it and live it. □ MAXIMILIAN KOLBE

Fr. John J. Hugo used to remind us that "He who says he has done enough has already perished. . ." and "You love God as much as the one you love the least." I recall his words often. He has been a great influence on the lives of our Catholic Workers.

Understanding God is not attained by calling into session all arguments for and against Him in order to debate whether He is a reality or a figment of the mind. God cannot be sensed as a second thought, as an explanation of the origin of the universe. He is either the first and last, or just another concept. Speculation does not precede faith. The antecedents of faith are the premise of wonder and the premise of praise. Worship of God precedes affirmation of His realness. We praise before we prove. We respond before we question. Proofs for the existence of God may add strength to our belief; they do not generate it. Human existence implies the realness of God. There is a certainty without knowledge in the depth of our being that accounts for our asking the ultimate question, a preconceptual certainty that lies beyond all formulation or verbalization. □ RABBI ABRAHAM JOSHUA HESCHEL

I listened to Richard Wagner's "Lohengrin" on the radio last night. Tom Hoey had been given eight tickets to the New York City Opera's production of "The Marriage of Figaro" - Deane Mowrer and others went. I prefer Wagner, pagan that he is.

I am still reading the works of George Orwell. Frank Sheed's wife, Maisie Ward, said she had found them so moving, so exciting, that she wept when she had finished them, in joyful gratitude and sorrow that there were no more of them to read.

May He support us all the day long,
till the shades lengthen, and the
evening comes, and the busy world
is hushed, and the fever of life is
over, and our work is done. Then in
His mercy may He give us a safe lodging,
and a holy rest, and peace at the last.
□ CARDINAL NEWMAN

About the Memorare . . . Sam Putnam, a Chicago city editor I worked for, gave me Huysmans' "En Retour" to read — the story of a man going to a convent every evening for Benediction of the Blessed Sacrament and hearing that prayer recited. I went from Chicago to New Orleans, to work on the New Orleans Item — lived in the square between the Cathedral (where I went to Benediction every evening) and the French market on the Mississippi River. This started my conversion. Having a baby a few years later finished it. I had her baptized, and began going to Mass myself. I received instruction from Sister Aloysia, a neighbor Sister of Charity.

*Reading Donald Attwater's Dictionary of the Saints again,
a Penguin paperback, and remembering Anatole France's
story of Thais and Paphinatius, a story of Egypt, I looked
it up and found it a true story. Mike Harank, one of our
workers in town, gave me this delightful book.*

Share everything with your brother. Do not say, "It
is private property." If you share what is everlasting,
you should be that much more willing to share things
which do not last. □ THE DIDACHE

The word of him who wishes to speak with men
without speaking to God is not fulfilled; but the word
of him who wishes to speak with God without speaking
with men goes astray. □ MARTIN BUBER

*"Doth it not irk me that upon the beach, the tides
monotonous run? Shall I not teach the sea some new
speech?" Who wrote it? Those lines came to mind when I
woke this morning. It certainly doesn't irk me! I love it
here. [at a cottage near the shore]*

Praying is better than drinking, and much more
pleasant to God. □ THOMAS MORE

Ruth Collins called. She is sending me down some Dorothy Sayers' mysteries. (I must re-read Dorothy Sayers' introductions to Dante.)

Saturday's Psalm 104 reminds me of Joseph and His Brethren by Thomas Mann, which Peter Maurin gave me to read (someone had given it to him). It also reminds me of the Potok books - My Name is Asher Lev, and others.

May I be no man's enemy, and may I be the friend of that which is eternal and abides. May I never quarrel with those nearest me; and if I do may I be quickly reconciled. May I devise no evil against any man and if any man devise evil against me may I escape unharmed and without the need to hurt him. May I love, seek and attain only that which is good. □ EUSEBIUS, BISHOP OF CAESAREA

Watched Leonard Bernstein on TV tonight, conducting the orchestra . . . whenever I watch an orchestra I always want to re-read The First Violin by Fothergill.

When I broke my arm at the age of twelve, Aunt Jenny, my mother's sister and my favorite aunt, sent me one Sherlock Holmes book a week, till I read them all.

There were excerpts from La Boheme this p.m. on radio —
my favorite opera in my twenties. Now I prefer Wagner.

Riches are like to those who hold them tightly; they
not only hinder a man, but pierce and wound him.
How many rich men of our day are clad in purple
-that is, in stuffs dyed with the sweat and blood of the
poor - because the clothes they wear are woven out of
theft, larcency, usury, and illegitimate gain! □ SAINT
ANTHONY

Deane Mowrer is going down to Washington, D.C. on
March 8th (1980) with a group from both houses, St.
Joseph's and Maryhouse, and from Peter Maurin Farm, to
vigil for a week at the Pentagon. I envy her vigor. Here I
sit 'on the shelf' and recall the Prayer of St. Ephraim
the Syrian:
    "Sorrow on me, beloved! that I unapt and reluctant in
my will abide, and behold, winter hath come upon me, and
the infinite tempest hath found me naked and spoiled and
with no perfecting of good in me. I marvel at myself, O
my beloved, how daily I default and daily do repent. I
build up for an hour and an hour overthrows what I have
built.
    "At evening I say, tomorrow I wll repent, but when
morning comes, joyous I waste the day. Again at evening I
say, I shall keep vigil all night and I shall entreat the Lord
to have mercy on my sins. But when the night is come, I
am full of sleep.

"Behold, those who received their talent along with me strive by day and night to trade with it, that they may win the word of praise and rule ten cities. But I, in my sloth, hid mine in the earth and my Lord makes haste to come, and behold, my heart trembles and I weep the day of my negligence and know not what excuse to bring. Have mercy upon me, Thou, Who alone art without sin, and save me, Who alone are pitiful and kind."

It would be ungrateful not to find enjoyment in my inactivity, not to "rejoice always" as the Psalmist said. Was it Ruskin who wrote about "the duty of delight"? What a nice phrase!

Whenever the general interest of any particular class suffers or is theatened with demands, which can in no other way be met, the public authority must step in to meet them. □ LEO XIII

St. Thomas Aquinas declared that for the practice of virtue, a certain amount of goods was indispensable . . . Cardinal Manning said that God's commandments could not be preached to men with empty stomachs. □ ABBE LUGAN

Help me, dear Lord, to do my little, daily tasks with "ease and discretion, with love and delight." I do not know where that quote comes from. It just popped into my head.

I must cultivate holy indifference. I should rejoice that I am "just an old woman," as the little boy said at a Rochester New York House of Hospitality dinner long ago. He said, "All day long they said 'Dorothy Day is coming,' and now she's here and she's just an old woman!" I certainly felt my age, not being able to get downstairs for Fr. Dan Berrigan's lecture on Thomas Merton. The auditorium was packed!

"I know not ugliness, it is a mood which has forsaken me." Where does that quote come from? Suddenly, these words had come into my mind this morning, while I enjoyed watching the rays of the sun rising over the East River, touching up the withered leaves on the little tree across the street. Later on the answer came. It was Max Bodenheim (long forgotten?) who recited it in that back room of the old saloon (which was the background for Eugene O'Neill's play, The Iceman Cometh) which many of us frequented those early days of Gene's career. His one-act plays were being put on at the Provincetown Playhouse, which was the downstairs "Little Theatre" on MacDougal Street (around the corner from Luke O'Connor's Tavern). Upstairs, Christine ran a restaurant. Her husband helped build the sets. The audience sat on benches. Gene's one-act plays were so engrossing that no-one minded the discomfort.

Seeing the O'Neill play Mourning Becomes Electra on television last night brought me back to those days when I frequented the Playhouse and felt Gene to be a playwright superior to Strindberg and Ibsen, the Scandinavian authors he much admired.

. . . And just a few Sundays ago we heard a little talk from a parish priest down in Staten Island. He was talking to the children about their posture in kneeling and the necessity for a vehement Amen to the final prayers said by the priest at the foot of the altar.

"Snap to it!" he had shouted right in the midst of those final prayers . . . And I thought sadly, if we waited to pray until we had the fervor of a saint we'd wait a long time.

The great Saint Teresa wrote in her autobiography of the thoughts like "little gnats" which buzz about by night here and there, and troubled her at her prayers. "Against this evil I know no remedy," she said. "The sole remedy which I meet with, after having wearied myself for many years is . . . to consider the memory no better than a mad man, and to leave it alone with its folly, for God alone can check its extravagances."

Tradition means giving votes to the most obscure of all classes, our ancestors. It is the democracy of the dead. Tradition refuses to submit to the small and arrogant oligarchy of those who merely happen to be walking about. All democrats object to men being disqualified by the accident of birth; tradition objects to their being disqualified by the accident of death.
☐ G. K. CHESTERTON

In Cleveland I was shaken out of my bed by the earthquake. The hotel I put up in, right near the terminal, was a tall narrow one and I was on the top floor. I was awakened by a fearful clattering of the window panes, the truly terrible noise of the elevator cables clanging and the smaller but just as ominous a noise of coat hangers clashing together in the closet. The whole hotel rocked as tho it were in a high wind and from all the rooms terrified occupants rushed out in their night clothes all the way down into the lobby. If it had not been for the distraction offered by Out of the Whirlwind by Wm. Joseph Walsh, an engrossing novel, I should have been hard put to it for the rest of the night to sleep. As it was I stayed up until three reading and then was able to fall asleep.

Lying on the couch while the chestnut logs snapped warmly in the big stove, I read Kagawa's 'Brotherhood Economics' which is one of the best and simplest accounts of the co-operative movement I have come across . . . I enjoyed reading his brief account of the mutual aid movement among the early Christians and communities of monks.

"A New Testament and a pair of knees are all one needs in jail," Fr. Hugo said to Harold Keane when he was sentenced to two and a half years in a federal prison after his application for conscientious objector status had been denied . . . I thought as I heard of this remark that there were quite a few things more that I would like to have in prison. Books for instance. As one of the old fathers of the desert said, "Prayer hath the travail of a mighty conflict to ones last breath." And to help in that travail there are always books . . . I need the books that I am reading now. For instance there is Gerald Vann. For the first time too I've seen Fr. Verner Moore's little book Prayer.

When Moses was leading his people out of the land of bondage he had as we all remember quite a time with Pharaoh. At the first concession Pharaoh made — that the Jews could leave provided they leave their gold and silver vessels for the temple behind - Moses said, "These things are necessary for the service of the Lord." That it seems to me is the attitude we must take towards our material possessions. And certainly we feel that books are necessary for the service of the Lord Our God.

Y ou who are fasting now in Lent. These are the men I bid you help. Clasp the afflicted man as if he were gold. Take the sufferer into your arms as if he were your own health, the welfare of your wife and children and all your house. Men shackled by illness, men cooped in some narrow lodging place or corner like Daniel in the den; these wait for you, the friend of the poor, to be another Habacuc to them.
☐ ST. GREGORY

It is hard to start learning how to relax or how to be efficient at housework at the age of fifty-four. The one thing one can keep starting over again to do is put first things first. To remember the primacy of the spiritual. To let the house go and just sit under the sky and breathe deeply for a while and pray one word over and over. "Short prayer," The Cloud of Unknowing advises: "Take thee a little word of one syllable . . . such a word is this word God or this word Love . . . and fasten this word to your heart so that it never go thence for anything that befalleth . . . This word shall be thy shield and thy spear . . . with this word thou shalt beat on this cloud and the darkness above thee. With this word thou shalt smite down all manner of thought under the cloud of forgetting. In as much that if any thought press upon thee to ask thee what though wouldst have, answer them with no more word but this word." . . . There can be silence, prayer, peace, in the midst of it all. If you practice at all.

Let us be servants in order to be leaders □ DOSTOIEVSKY

My reading during the past few months mostly during travelling, whether by train, bus or subway was The Family (novel) by Federova; True Devotion by de Monfort; Graham Greene and Sigrid Undset; Darkness at Noon by Koestler; Raissa Maritain's story of her and Jacques' student days and their friendships; Jacques St. Paul.

Perhaps we are called sentimental because we speak of love. We say love our president, our country. We say that we love our enemies too. "Hell," said Bernanos, "is not to love anymore." . . . "Love is an exchange of gifts," St. Ignatius said. Love is a breaking of bread. Remember the story of Christ meeting his disciples at Emmaus . . . Love is not the starving of whole populations. Love is not the

SAINT PAUL

bombardment of open cities. Love is not killing; it is the laying down of one's life for one's friend. Hear Fr. Zossima in the Brothers Karamazov:

"Love one another, Fathers," he said, speaking to his monks. "Love God's people. Because we have come here and shut ourselves within these walls, we are no holier than those that are outside, but on the contrary, from the very fact of coming here, each of us has confessed to himself that he is worse than others, than all men on earth . . . And the longer the monk lives in his seclusion, the more keenly he must recognize that. Else he would have no reason to come here.
 When he realizes that he is not only worse than others, but that he is responsible to all men for all and everything, for all human sins, national and individual, only then the aim of our seclusion is attained . . . Each of you keep watch over your heart and confess your sins unceasingly
. . Hate not the atheists, the teachers of evil, the materialists . . . hate not even the wickedness. Remember them in your prayers thus: Save, O Lord, all those who have none to pray for them; save, too, all those who will not pray. And add, it is not in pride that I make this prayer, O Lord, for I am lower than all men . . ."

We Have Been Friends Together is a book which I must keep talking about, it is so lovely, so stimulating. It is the story of Raissa Maritain's life, first in Russia then in France, her early schooldays, her meeting with Jacques, who became her husband, and their friends Charles Peguy and Leon Bloy. The story takes us up to their conversion . . . I have been so fascinated by this book that I carried it about for days and could not bear to loan it to anyone.

A cup of coffee never tastes so good as when coming out of an ice cold room into a warm kitchen.